WEBSITES FROM A TO Z

JOHN COWPERTWAIT

D0808825

ICON BOOKS UK
TOTEM BOOKS USA

Published in the UK in 2002
by Icon Books Ltd., Grange Road,
Duxford, Cambridge CB2 4QF
e-mail: info@iconbooks.co.uk
www.iconbooks.co.uk

Published in the USA in 2002
by Totem Books
Inquiries to: Icon Books Ltd.,
Grange Road, Duxford, Cambridge,
CB2 4QF, UK

Sold in the UK, Europe, South Africa
and Asia by Faber and Faber Ltd.,
3 Queen Square, London WC1N 3AU
or their agents

Distributed to the trade In the USA
by National Book Network Inc.,
4720 Boston Way, Lanham,
Maryland 20706

Distributed in the UK, Europe,
South Africa and Asia by
Macmillan Distribution Ltd.,
Houndmills, Basingstoke RG21 6XS

Distributed in Canada by
Penguin Books Canada,
10 Alcorn Avenue, Suite 300,
Toronto, Ontario M4V 3B2

Published in Australia in 2002
by Allen & Unwin Pty. Ltd.,
PO Box 8500, 83 Alexander Street,
Crows Nest, NSW 2065

ISBN 1 84046 347 3

Text copyright © 2002 John Cowpertwait

The author has asserted his moral rights.

Typesetting and artwork by Wayzgoose

Printed and bound in the UK
by Cox & Wyman Ltd., Reading

WEBSITES FROM A TO Z

Waiver

The information in this book is provided for guidance purposes only. All the information contained within this book is believed to be correct at the time of going to press. However, the author or the publishers cannot be held responsible for any errors, omissions or factual inaccuracies.

Websites come and Websites go. Their purpose and content, and their Web addresses can and do change frequently. Each Website mentioned in this book has been checked prior to publication; however, some changes may have occurred by the time you read this book. This is beyond the control of the author and the publisher.

Websites are included in this book as examples only and inclusion should not be taken as an endorsement of the contents of Websites. The views expressed within Websites referenced in this book are entirely independent of the author and the publisher.

Thanks

Thanks again to Jocelyne Dudding for her advice and comments, to Simon Flynn for his hard work and patience, and to everyone else who showed an interest.

Profile

The author has worked with information technology for over two decades. He was a senior manager with leading companies in the software industry for many years and ran his own marketing company. He is now a marketing advisor for businesses and arts organisations, and occasionally lectures at the Department of Arts Policy and Management, City University, London. He is co-author of the best-selling book *The Internet from A to Z*, also from Icon Books.

Companion Book

This is a companion book to *The Internet from A to Z*, an easy to use reference guide which introduces the Internet and the World Wide Web more fully, and provides explanations of over 1,000 Internet-related terms in an A to Z format.

CONTENTS

Transport 295

PART ONE

Websites from A to Z

Websites from A to Z is designed to make accessible the rich reservoir of information and resources that is available through the Web. It is for those who want to make intelligent use of the Internet.

The book covers a range of sites encompassing a variety of subjects, including the arts, food and drink, gardening, health and sport. Sites have also been incorporated that address issues not found in most Website listing books, such as specific health matters, human rights, media issues, globalisation and environmental concerns.

Part of the Internet's great appeal is the international perspective it can bring, and sites from different countries to our own can often provide valuable alternative views and opinions. Reflecting this, we've listed English-language sites from a number of countries, including Australia, New Zealand, Canada, the USA, South Africa, the UK and Ireland. Many of these sites can also be read in languages other than English.

Using this Book

For *Websites from A to Z*, independent thinking is important. This publication is not sponsored by anyone, it does not carry advertising, there are no false sites knowingly listed, and no payment of any kind has been made by sites to be listed here.

Sections

The book is divided into two sections:

Part One briefly introduces the Internet and the World Wide Web, and provides guidance about searching for Websites and bookmarking Webpages.

Part Two lists over 3,000 interesting sites selected from the many tens of thousands seen during the compilation of this book. The sites are divided into subject sections, listed alphabetically.

Links

In Part Two, links have been made between sections of this book that are related. For example, the 'Health' section is linked with the 'Elderly and Ageing' section, which is located in the 'Environmental Issues and World Concerns' section. This particular link is shown as

Links: Environmental Issues and World Concerns/Elderly and Ageing

at the end of the Health section, p. 177. Other links appear throughout the book.

Top 200 Favourite Websites

There are more than 3,000 sites listed in *Websites from A to Z*, and from them around 200 have been selected. We particularly liked these sites for one reason or another. They are indicated in the text throughout by a **❻** icon. These sites may make a useful starting point for anyone who wishes to explore the many different aspects of the Web.

Websites and the Web

The Internet vs. the World Wide Web

It's worth making a simple distinction between the Web and the Internet.

The Web, or World Wide Web to give its full title, is the multimedia functionality of the Internet. It's the vehicle for Websites, the place where information in the form of text, graphics, animation, sound or moving images resides.

The Internet is the international series of linked networks, comprising wires, cables and satellite connections over which this information is conveyed, and which permits a series of data connection services to operate. These services include e-mail, newsgroups, file transfer services, and the World Wide Web. Since about 1994, the Web has become the dominant part of the Net, as it is more accessible and easier to master for the majority of users than the other services, which require a higher degree of technical ability and awareness.

Web Browser

To enter and navigate the Web, users require a Web browser, usually Internet Explorer or Netscape Navigator. Internet Explorer is owned by Microsoft and is distributed with Windows, the operating system found on the majority of computers. Netscape Navigator is the most widely used alternative and was recently purchased by the Internet service provider AOL. Other browsers exist, such as Opera (www.opera.com) and NeoPlanet (www.neoplanet.com), but are used by significantly fewer people.

For a more detailed explanation of Web browsers see *The Internet from A to Z*, from Icon Books.

Websites

This book is primarily concerned with Websites. These are the places where material is freely published on the World Wide Web by companies, corporations, organisations, groups, or individuals, and which are usually open to anyone connected to the Web.

Websites have become increasingly sophisticated in the past few years. The Web was originally conceived as a means of transferring hypertext documents between researchers. The earliest Websites were essentially text-based, with the occasional addition of basic static graphical images.

Once public access to the Web became more widespread, the number of Websites began to grow. Initially Websites were often used merely as posting boards to publish static information, such as personal diaries, commercial products and services details, events information, or to share data between a group of individuals, perhaps in the form of a newsletter. Photographic images were often incorporated into these sites.

As the multimedia potential of the Web started to be realised, music sites established by fans began to post digital music files which could be transferred from one computer to another, and radio stations began broadcasting over the Web. Websites generally became more sophisticated with the development of animation products and the arrival of a much wider choice of the media players necessary to access digital sound and images.

As faster broadband connections have become more common, the movement of data consisting of sound and moving images, both from archives and in real-time, has become commonplace. Much of the technology in this area was originally driven by the porn industry, which was one of the first commercial sectors to utilise the ability of the Web to make available downloadable short movie or video clips. This aspect of the Web has been harnessed with serious intent in the last few years by media conglomerates as a means of making mainstream movies and music available to everyone with the right level of connection.

Websites Today

Today Websites consist of anything from a few pages posted by an individual to huge corporate sites incorporating video and audio, discussion forums, and Websites within Websites.

Early adopters of the Web, such as the BBC, were quick to spot the revolution that was happening, as the Web became an alternative broadcast medium. Now these early adopters have huge Websites with hundreds of individual Webpages subdivided into many subsites. Subsites are denoted by the stem division in the Web address (also known as the URL, or Uniform Resource Locator); for example, www.bbc.co.uk/arts or bbc.co.uk/health.

A forward slash denotes a division in a Website. The arts or health section of the BBC Website can be reached directly by keying in the URL with the forward slash and subsite title, or indirectly via the home page at www.bbc.co.uk.

Websites are typically entered via the homepage, the starting point from which the remaining subsections and pages of the Website can be located. A typical Website home page looks similar to the BBC Online homepage.

Other sections of the site are found by clicking on one of the navigation buttons, which are typically located in a row across the top of the screen or in a column down the left-hand side, although this convention is increasingly being forsaken. Where no immediate navigational aids are apparent, passing the cursor over icons or images may change the cursor from an arrow into a small hand icon, which indicates that other pages can be reached by clicking the right mouse button.

For a more detailed explanation of Website structure, see *The Internet from A to Z*, from Icon Books.

Looking for Clues

Two useful areas to be found within Websites are 'About' and 'Sitemaps'. Although in many ways peripheral to the main sections of Websites, these can provide useful information.

'Sitemap' pages are sometimes available in large sites, where navigating a route through the pages can become complicated. The sitemap provides a single-page overview of the whole site, often in the form of an organisation chart. The user can get a feel for the total contents of the site and click directly onto the section or subsite they wish to visit, without having to make their way through layers of other pages. Another common means of going directly to a subsite is by an A–Z index, such as that provided at www.bbc.co.uk/a–z.

It may be important to know details about the origins of the Website, for instance, about the companies or individuals that fund it, or the objectives of the site. 'About' pages may supply this information, in the form of a kind of background footnote. The 'About' section link can often be found within the navigation bar or column of the homepage of a Website, or at the base of the homepage. However, 'About' sections are also often found via other routes; for example, www.bbc.co.uk/info is found by scrolling through the Main Sites box on the BBC A–Z page and clicking on 'About BBC'.

The Web is a highly dynamic environment and, over time, Websites may move to new addresses or they may simply be abandoned. While the style of a site will sometimes indicate whether it has been recently updated or is in regular use, it can sometimes be difficult to assess how current or live a site is. Another short, but extremely useful, piece of information is the 'site last updated on xx.xx.xx' phrase that can occasionally be found, usually at the end of the first Webpage. This should give some indication as to how up-to-date the information on the site is. Unfortunately, this phrase appears all too infrequently, and other clues may have to be sought as to the current validity of the information.

Browsing the Web

You'll sometimes find things you don't expect when surfing the Web, including the following:

'The page cannot be displayed'

One of the pages you will come across most frequently when using the Internet is the one shown on page 22. It appears when the Webpage you are trying to reach cannot be found. There may be a number of reasons for this, including an overload on the server storing the page you want. However, the most likely reason why you will come across this message is that the Webpage you wish to access no longer exists and has been removed from the server. This could occur because the information it contained is no longer deemed to be relevant. Alternatively, the information may have been re-sited within the Website. This happens when sites have been streamlined or redesigned to make the information more navigable. The site may also have ceased to exist and been taken down in its entirety, or it may now be reached by a different URL.

Sometimes the second paragraph of the message will suggest that you try a shortened version of the address. You can usually click on this address within the body of the message to be taken to that page, which will usually be the homepage of the site. However, clicking on the address is no guarantee that you will reach the site.

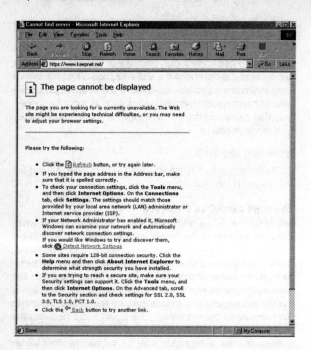

Splash Pages

These are the screens that pre-empt a Website homepage. A splash page may be a simple static page asking the user to click to enter the site, or it may be a page asking you to select which language you wish the site to be in, or to ensure that you have a particular media player installed, for example.

Increasingly, animated Flash sequences appear before the user is admitted into the main body of a site. These sequences can be accompanied by music or other sounds and, if you are on a fast connection, they may make a startling impression. However, more often than not, on a slow-speed connection they will take some time to load and the effect will be undermined. In these cases the 'Skip Intro' button that usually appears towards the right-hand side of the screen will prove a useful option to bypass these potentially time consuming, cosmetic additions to sites.

Pop-ups

Screens of varying sizes may pop-up as you are entering or navigating a site. These frequently contain special offers or advertisements, and can prove counter-productive to both the host site and the companies who are being advertised, as they are often extremely intrusive and annoying.

Bookmarks and Favorites

Some of the Websites you visit will prove particularly useful or enjoyable, and you will want to visit them again. Bookmarking is the method provided within the browser to save the effort of remembering or noting the URL, or searching afresh each time you want to locate the site.

Bookmarks and Favorites are two different words describing the same thing: Webpage addresses (or URLs) that have been saved and filed within the browser for repeat viewing.

Even though Internet Explorer is by far the most used browser, the term used within it, 'Favorites', is less commonly used for the Webpage addresses you save than the Netscape term 'Bookmarks'. The word 'Bookmark' is used both substantively and imperatively – you will see Websites imploring you to 'bookmark this site', encouraging you to save the address reference in order to make it easy to return regularly to the site, regardless of whether you save it as a Favorite or as a Bookmark.

How to Bookmark a Webpage

Bookmarking is a simple procedure that in the long run will probably save you lots of time, and will ensure that any Webpages of interest that you visit are always readily available. In Internet Explorer there are two simple ways to save a Favorite, or, in other words, to make a Bookmark, when you have a Webpage onscreen that you wish to save:

1. a) Click on the Favorites button located towards the centre of the third row of your browser window. The icon is shaped like a file.

   b) This will bring up a column of your Favorites on the left-hand side of your screen. You will see two options at the top of the column – Add or Organise.

   c) Select Add by clicking on it. A smaller window will appear called Add Favorite. The name or description allocated to the particular Webpage by the Web-designer will appear in the Name box. Note that this is not always the same as the URL, and is often, but not always, a description of the contents of the page. This name appears in the Favorites listings, and you may wish to change the name allocated to one of your own, which may help you recognise the site more readily.

   If it's the site as a whole that you are interested in, rather than just one of the pages within it, then saving the home-page is probably the best option, as the home-page URL is more likely to remain constant, whereas the URL for individual pages may change over time as Websites are reorganised.

   d) To add the Webpage to your Favorite list, click on the OK button at the top of the right of the small screen. Your Favorite should now have been added. This means that when you next want to reach the site, rather than having to search for it again, or remember the address, you simply enter your Favorites folder, click on the Website address and the Webpage will be opened.

e) When you have added a number of Websites to your Favorites list, you will want to organise them into groups so you can locate the sites easily. They will probably fall into natural groupings which you can gather together in folders. To create a folder, press the New Folder button at the bottom of the right-hand column on the right-hand side of the small Add Favorite window. Then name the folder and add the file to it.

f) You can also create folders within folders by pressing the Folder button when you are already in a folder, to produce an organisational hierarchy for your bookmarked Favorites. You can reorganise the Favorites within the folders at any time by clicking on the Organise button and following the instructions. Alternatively, Favorites can also be organised within the Favorites list column: they can be moved by positioning the cursor over the Favorite, holding down the right mouse button and, using the cursor, moving the Favorite to the folder in which it is to be relocated, and releasing the mouse button.

g) A small toggle box in the Add Favorites window invites you to make the Favorites readable offline ('Make available offline'). If you select this option, the page will be saved to the hard disk of your computer, which enables you to read the pages you select even when you are no longer logged-on to the Web.

2. There is a second way to save or bookmark Favorites:

a) Assuming Internet Explorer is at default settings, you will see on the second row of your browser window the word Favorites, this time without an icon. Click on the word Favorites towards the top left of your screen, above the row of buttons.

b) This will bring up a drop-down box showing the folders in your current list. Clicking on the Add to Favorites option will bring up the Add Favorites box as above. To add Favorites follow from c) above.

The process of Bookmarking may sound a little complicated, but once you've done it a couple of times, it will be a natural process. Try it a few times and see.

Looking at Bookmarks and Favorites

To look at saved Favorites, click on either the Favorites icon or the word Favorites. Clicking on the icon will open up the favorites column, and clicking on each folder will open up a list of the contents vertically underneath the folder title. Clicking on the folder title again will shrink the folders.

An alternative way of looking at Favorites is to click on the word Favorite, which will bring the Favorites folders onscreen as a drop-down column. Passing the cursor over each of the folders will result in a cascade column appearing to the right of the box showing the contents of each folder.

To open up a site, click on the chosen Favorite. If you have saved the Favorite to be readable when working offline, and you are doing so, the last version of the Website used will be shown. If you are working online, the current version will appear.

Searching the Net

Web-based search engines and directories are a means of locating sites on the Internet. Each has its own search criteria and style of presenting the results, usually known as the hit list.

When using Web-based search facilities, people are usually doing one of two things: they are searching either specifically or generally. Specific searches are performed when users are looking for one site that they know exists, but for which they don't know the Website address (URL), for example, the official Website of Manchester United Football Club. General searches are performed when the user is seeking to gain a general list of Website addresses relating to a particular topic, for example, a list of Websites concerned with soccer.

There are two types of search resources on the Web – the search engine and the directory. A lot of crossover between the two types exists, as directories will also offer searches, and many search engines segment their searches into broad subject areas, such as sport, for example.

Directories present a list of categories, for example 'Shopping', or 'Arts', or 'Sports'. These categories can be subdivided many times until you reach a narrow category in which the group of sites or specific site may be found; for example, Sports, Soccer, Soccer Teams, Soccer Teams UK. At each sub-stage you can perform a search in the narrow category. So it is likely that searching for 'Manchester United' at the Soccer Teams stage will produce a list containing a number of sites to choose from, probably comprising a series of independent fan sites and commercial merchandise or tickets sites, plus somewhere near the top of the hit list, the official Manchester United Website.

Search engines operate differently, in that you enter a key word or words that will help locate the site you are looking for without first narrowing down the search by subject. Keying-in 'Manchester United' should take you directly to a hit list either containing sites which contain the phrase 'Manchester United' or sites for which the words 'Manchester United' are key words. Key words are provided by Website operators to search engines for each site as an aid to searching.

Keying-in the words 'Manchester' and 'united' would result in a slightly different set of results, comprising sites which contain the words 'Manchester' and 'united', but not necessarily one after the other as a phrase. However, it is likely that both methods would enable the official Manchester United Website to be located without too much difficulty.

Some search engines work better on a small number of focused words, others on a greater number of words. Depending on the search engine you use and its limitations and range, you may find that keying in 'Manchester United' and 'official website' will produce a hit list with the official Manchester United Website at the top. In terms of quantity, the broader the term used, the more sites are likely to be delivered. For example, it is likely that 'Manchester United' will deliver a longer list than 'Manchester United official website'.

Many URLs are instinctive and obvious, as is the URL for the official Manchester United site, www.manutd.com. An alternative method of locating this site, and sites like it, may be to make an informed guess and attempt to locate the site by directly keying in an estimate or estimations of the site's URL into the address bar on the browser and pressing the return or enter key. If the guess is correct, you will be taken there directly.

It is worth remembering that all Web-based directories and search engines offer searches of only a section of the Web. Out of the millions of sites out there, only a proportion may be reached by each search engine. This is why it is important, especially when doing general rather than specific searches, not to limit searches to only one search engine or directory. By doing so you are restricting your reach across the Internet and you may not reach the site you want, or catch as broad a range of sites for a specific theme or topic as you are seeking.

There are many different free-to-use search engine portal sites available. Some of these use similar search technologies and subsequently may give a similar hit list. Others use differing search technologies and will deliver results different to each other. Search engines use different search methods and criteria. If you are having difficulty locating sites, it's worth investigating how the searches are conducted by looking at the Help or Advanced Search Features sections of the search engine.

Search engines can search subsections of the Web, such as countries and regions. So, for example, Yahoo has search engine Websites specifically for Australia and New Zealand, the UK, and other locations. Local searches can be made from these sites, and each site can also search across the Web, regardless of country zones.

For some of the best search engines see WebStuff, Search Engines in Part Two.

PART TWO

Website Directory

This section includes many of our favourite Websites. However, bear in mind that just as no Web-based search engine or directory can ever hope to cover all the sites on the Web, no book of this type can ever hope to be totally comprehensive. For each subsection that follows, there are hundreds, possibly thousands, more sites. However, we've selected some of the best to serve as an introduction to the huge wealth of quality information and resources that are available via the Internet.

Arts

Websites are now an integral part of the communications strategies of arts institutions, and the majority of the major arts centres, galleries and museums of the world have Websites of varying degrees of complexity. At their simplest these sites tend to provide just a static non-interactive brief overview of collections, together with opening hours and location details.

However, at their most sophisticated, museums and gallery sites provide huge amounts of information, with archive material, features and articles, and fully searchable online catalogues of their collections. Such sites are regularly updated to provide accurate information relating to changing displays and exhibitions, and often provide frequent e-mail communications about forthcoming events and activities.

GENERAL ARTS

The sites in this overview section relate to venues, listings, and sources of reference and research information that cater to the arts generally.

Arts listings

The sites below are mainly general portal sites that contain or link to details of all the arts, including dance, theatre, spoken and written word, music and museums.

WORLDWIDE
www.whatsonwhen.com
International arts, cultural and general events for cities across the world.

NATIONAL
Australia
www.cultureandarts.wa.gov.au
Arts and culture of Western Australia.

Canada
www.artscanadian.com
The Canadian Cultural Web directory links to dance and theatre companies and galleries.

South Africa
www.artslink.co.za
Culture and entertainment hub, including news, discussion and events calendar.

United Kingdom
www.artsonline.com
Arts Council of England general arts portal.

United States
www.culturefinder.com
State-by-state nationwide search for theatre, music, opera and visual arts events.

Arts centres

NATIONAL

Australia
www.afct.org.au
The Adelaide Festival Centre.

www.brisbanepowerhouse.com
The Brisbane Powerhouse.

www.qpat.com.au
Queensland Performing Arts Centre.

www.soh.nsw.gov.au
The Sydney Opera House, Australia's prestigious venue for classical music, dance and musical performances, as well as opera.

www.vicartscentre.com.au
Melbourne's arts complex.

Canada

www.nac-cna.ca
Ottawa's National Arts Centre, venue for English and French theatre, classical music, and dance.

United Kingdom

www.arnolfini.demon.co.uk
Located in Bristol's harbourside, the Arnolfini is one of Europe's leading centres for the contemporary arts.

www.balticmill.com
BALTIC is the major new international centre for contemporary visual art, situated in Gateshead in the North East of England.

www.barbican.org.uk
The Barbican Centre near the City of London is Europe's largest multi-arts and conference venue, and is home to the London Symphony Orchestra and the Royal Shakespeare Company.

www.sbc.org.uk
London's South Bank Centre includes the Royal Festival Hall and the Hayward Gallery.

United States

kennedy-center.org
John F. Kennedy Center for the Performing Arts, Washington DC.

www.walkerart.org
The Walker Art Center, Minneapolis.

Arts reference and research

There is a plenitude of arts education resources on the Web, with vast amounts of material reachable by searchable databases and directories. The following sites provide extensive links to Websites about subjects across the arts.

adam.ac.uk/index.html
ADAM is the Art, Design, Architecture and Media searchable information gateway aimed at the UK's higher education community, but accessible by all.

iberia.vassar.edu/ifla-idal
Searchable database of around 3,000 libraries and library departments with holdings in art, architecture and archaeology.

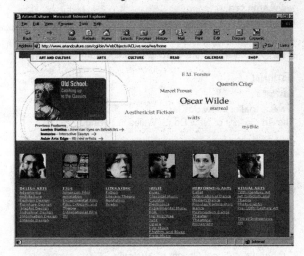

www.artandculture.com
Impressive well designed encyclopaedic overview of arts and culture. **⑤**

www.zeroland.co.nz
There are some good links indexed in this directory overview of international culture from New Zealand.

ART

The sites in this section relate primarily to the visual arts, and museums of modern art are included here, rather than in the following museums section. Use these sites to find information about gallery collections, temporary exhibitions and displays, talks and events, gallery location and opening hours.

Art galleries

WORLDWIDE

www.amn.org
Art Museum Network.

www.excalendar.net
Exhibition calendar of the world's leading art museums.**❻**

NATIONAL

Australia

www.artgallery.nsw.gov.au
The Art Gallery of New South Wales in Sydney.

www.artgallery.sa.gov.au
The Art Gallery of Southern Australia in Adelaide.

www.artnow.org.au
Australian Centre for Contemporary Art, Melbourne, Victoria.

www.mca.com.au
Flash site of the Museum of Contemporary Art, Sydney.

www.nga.gov.au
Canberra's National Gallery of Australia.

www.ngv.vic.gov.au
The National Gallery of Victoria, Melbourne, is the oldest public art gallery in Australia.

www.qag.qld.gov.au
Queensland Art Gallery in Brisbane.

Canada

Alberta

www.artgallerycalgary.org
The Art Gallery of Calgary displays contemporary art.

British Columbia

aggv.bc.ca
The Art Gallery of Greater Victoria has a permanent collection of over 15,000 objects.

www.galleries.bc.ca
Portal site for all the public art galleries of the interior of British Columbia.

www.vanartgallery.bc.ca
Vancouver Art Gallery.

Ontario

national.gallery.ca
The National Gallery of Canada, Ottawa.

www.ago.net
The Art Gallery of Ontario, Toronto.

www.portraits.gc.ca
The Portrait Gallery of Canada, Ottawa.

www.thepowerplant.org
The Power Plant, Toronto, is Canada's leading contemporary art gallery.

Quebec

www.macm.org
Museum of Contemporary Art, Montreal.

www.mdq.org
The Musée de Quebec, Quebec's National Art Gallery.

www.mmfa.qc.ca
Montreal Museum of Fine Arts.

Ireland
www.hughlane.ie
The Hugh Lane Gallery, Dublin, new home of Francis Bacon's studio.

www.modernart.ie
The Irish Museum of Modern Art, Dublin.

www.nationalgallery.ie
The National Gallery of Ireland, Dublin.

New Zealand
nz.art.coca.org.nz
Centre of Contemporary Art, Christchurch.

www.akcity.govt.nz/around/places/artgallery/index.html
Auckland Art Gallery.

www.christchurchartgallery.org.nz
The new Christchurch Art Gallery.

www.city-gallery.org.nz
Wellington City Art Gallery.

www.mcdougall.org.nz
The Robert McDougall Art Gallery, Christchurch.

South Africa
www.museums.org.za/sang
South African National Gallery, Cape Town.

United Kingdom
London
www.barbican.org.uk/art
Barbican Art provides an adventurous series of exhibitions at its two main galleries housed within the Barbican Arts Centre in the City of London. ❻

www.dulwichpicturegallery.org.uk
The UK's oldest picture gallery.

www.hayward-gallery.org.uk
Temporary exhibitions are staged at this gallery in the South Bank complex.

www.hermitagerooms.com
The Hermitage Rooms at Somerset House house temporary displays from the namesake museum in St Petersburg.

www.nationalgallery.org.uk
The UK National Gallery houses one of the greatest collections of European paintings.

www.npg.org.uk
National Portrait Gallery in Trafalgar Square has representations of the rich, the powerful and the influential.

www.royalacademy.org.uk
The Royal Academy of Arts in Piccadilly shows high profile temporary exhibitions.

www.serpentinegallery.org.uk
This former tearoom in Kensington Gardens hosts some of the most popular small exhibitions in London.

www.somerset-house.org.uk
Somerset House, an impressive 18th century building recently renovated to house the Gilbert Collection of decorative art and the Hermitage Rooms, also includes The Courtauld Institute of Art which boasts one of Britain's finest collections of Impressionist and post-Impressionist works.**❻**

www.tate.org.uk
The Tate Website provides information about all the Tate Gallery's branches: Britain, Modern, Liverpool and St Ives, as well as offering online shopping facilities and an online searchable catalogue of 25,000 works.**❻**

www.the-wallace-collection.org.uk
A fine collection of paintings, porcelain, furniture and armoury.

www.whitechapel.org
Historic venue for temporary art exhibitions in the heart of London's East End.

Regional art galleries
www.artatwalsall.org.uk
Unusual site from the New Art Gallery at Walsall.

www.bmag.org.uk
Details of Birmingham's Central Museum and Art Gallery and other local museums.

www.cityartgalleries.org.uk
Details of Manchester's art galleries, including the City Art Gallery.

www.henry-moore-fdn.co.uk
Details of the Henry Moore Institute, Leeds.

www.moma.org.uk
Museum of Modern Art, Oxford.

www.natgalscot.ac.uk
The National Galleries of Scotland site provides details about the Scottish National Gallery, the Scottish Portrait Gallery, the Scottish Gallery of Modern Art and the Dean Gallery.

www.wolverhamptonart.org.uk
The recently refurbished Wolverhampton Art Gallery.

United States
California
www.famsf.org
The Fine Arts Museum of San Francisco.

www.getty.edu/museum
The J. Paul Getty Museum, Los Angeles.

www.moca-la.org
The Museum of Contemporary Art, Los Angeles.

www.nortonsimon.org
The Norton Simon Museum, Pasadena.

www.sfmoma.org
San Francisco Museum of Modern Art.

Illinois
www.artic.edu
The Art Institute of Chicago.

www.mcachicago.org
Museum of Contemporary Art, Chicago.

Massachusetts
www.gardnermuseum.org
The Isabella Stewart Gardner Museum, Boston.

www.mfa.org
Museum of Fine Arts, Boston.

Michigan
www.dia.org
The Detroit Institute of Fine Arts.

New Mexico
www.okeeffemuseum.org
The Georgia O'Keeffe Museum.

New York
www.brooklynart.org
Brooklyn Museum of Art.

www.diacenter.org
Dia Center for the Arts.

www.frick.org
The Frick Collection.

www.guggenheim.org
Entry point for the Guggenheim's art empire, covering
galleries in New York, Bilbao, Venice, Berlin and Las Vegas.

www.metmuseum.org
The Metropolitan Museum of Art, near Central Park.

www.moma.org
The influential Museum of Modern Art.🄵

www.whitney.org
The Whitney Museum of American Art.

Washington DC
hirshhorn.si.edu
The Smithsonian Hirshhorn Museum and Sculpture Gardens.

www.nga.gov
National Gallery of Art.

www.nmaa.si.edu
The Smithsonian American Art Museum.

www.npg.si.edu
Smithsonian National Portrait Gallery.

www.phillipscollection.org
The Phillips Collection, America's first museum of modern art.

Art news and listings

Many of these sites provide e-mail bulletin services to inform
registered users about private views, art auctions, openings
and exhibition schedules.

WORLDWIDE
www.absolutearts.com
International art news.

www.artcult.com
Independent worldwide listings of sculpture parks.

www.artrepublic.com
Exhibitions details around the world and gallery links. 🄵

www.artupdate.com
Fortnightly e-mail and Website listings of international art exhibitions.

www.theartnewspaper.com
Website that emulates the look and feel of the highly respected monthly. 🄵

Moroni's "The tailor", on view at the Nationalmuseum in Stockholm until 7 January (click here for article)

www.thegallerychannel.com
Tailor art and exhibition news to your own tastes at the
Gallery Channel.

Other worldwide sites

hydra-island.com
www.artdaily.com
www.art-online.org
www.artupdate.com

NATIONAL

Canada

www.artistsincanada.com
Portal to art in Canada, covering artists, galleries and art
resources.

South Africa

www.coartnews.co.za
Useful review of South Africa's contemporary art scene.🅕

United Kingdom

www.artguide.org
Artist, museum and exhibition guide for UK and Ireland.

www.newexhibitions.com
Straightforward and comprehensive UK art exhibition
guide.

United States

www.artswire.org
Weekly arts news from the New York Foundation for the Arts.

www.galleryguide.org
US commercial gallery guide, searchable by state.

Buying art

Many traditional commercial galleries now have Websites. However, space does not permit them to be listed here. Most of the following sites are online galleries, or galleries with a strong online presence.

INTERNATIONAL

www.artist-info.com

NATIONAL

South Africa

www.african-artist.co.za
www.vgallery.co.za

United Kingdom

www.artlondon.com
www.art-online.org
www.britart.com
www.eyestorm.com
www.multiplestore.org

United States

www.artcnet.com
www.artnet.com
www.artsofar.com

Art magazines

www.artforum.com
Well designed site from New York's art magazine.🅕

www.artmonthly.co.uk
UK's *Art Monthly*.

www.artmonthly.org.au
Australia's *Art Monthly*.

www.artnews.co.nz
Online edition of New Zealand's quarterly arts publication.

www.artnewsonline.com
New York art journal.

www.frieze.com
UK magazine of contemporary art and culture.

www.tatemag.com
Online version of *Tate* magazine, associated with the UK gallery of the same name.

Art reference and research

www.aesthetics-online.org
The American Society for Aesthetics site with good links.

www.artchive.com
Some useful information, including theory and criticism, at this interestingly designed site.

www.artcyclopedia.com
Fine Arts Search Engine with links to 700 arts sites.

www.artlex.com
Art dictionary of more than 3,000 visual culture terms.

www.fineartindex.co.uk
UK art directory, including exhibition guide.

www.groveart.com
Subscribe online to the *Grove Dictionary of Art*.

www.temple.edu/jaac
Journal of Aesthetics and Arts Criticism.

MUSEUMS

Here's our selection from the vast number of museum Websites.

Worldwide

www.icom.org/vlmp
The International Council of Museums' Virtual Library

museums pages provide extensive unfussy links to art gallery and museum sites around the world.**F**

www.musee-online.org
US-based directory of art galleries and museums of all types worldwide.

National

AUSTRALIA

General information
amol.org.au
Australian Art Museums and Galleries Online portal.

Museums
www.amonline.net.au
Australia Museum, Sydney, established 1827.

www.museum.vic.gov.au
The gateway Website of Victoria's state museum which runs four individual museums, including the Scienceworks Museum, the Immigration Museum and the Melbourne Museum.

www.museum.wa.gov.au
Details of the six branches of the Western Australia Museum, including the main site at Perth.

www.nma.gov.au
National Museum of Australia, Canberra.

CANADA
General information
www.virtualmuseum.ca
The Virtual Museum of Canada is an online exhibition project involving many of Canada's museums. Also includes the Find a Museum directory.

Museums

Ontario

www.rom.on.ca
The Royal Ontario Museum, Toronto.

www.warmuseum.ca
The Canadian War Museum, Ottawa.

Quebec

www.mcq.org
Museum of Civilisation and the Musée de l'Amérique Français.

IRELAND

www.museum.ie
The National Museum of Ireland.

NEW ZEALAND

General information

www.nzmuseums.co.nz
Guide to museums, art galleries and national treasures.

Museums

www.tepapa.govt.nz
Te Papa Tongarewa, New Zealand's new National Museum, Wellington.

SOUTH AFRICA

General information

www.museums.org.za
Searchable portal to the museums and galleries of South Africa.

Museums

www.museums.org.za/sam
The South African Museum, Cape Town.

www.nasmus.co.za
National Museum, Bloemfontein.

www.robben-island.org.za
A former prison, Robben Island is now a museum reflecting the past uses of the Island and its natural history.

UNITED KINGDOM

General information

www.24hourmuseum.org.uk
News and feature information portal covering museums and galleries in England and Wales, including the Museum Finder directory.

www.icom.org/vlmp/uk.html
Excellent links to UK museum sites.

www.museums.co.uk
UK museums knowledge base, searchable alphabetically and by region or name of museum.

www.nmgw.ac.uk
National Museums and Galleries of Wales.

www.nms.ac.uk
National Museums of Scotland.

Museums

London

www.freud.org.uk
Learn about the father of modern psychoanalysis at The Freud Museum.

www.iwm.org.uk
The Imperial War Museum site provides links to its network of national museums.

www.museumoflondon.org.uk
London from prehistoric times to the present day.

www.nhm.ac.uk
The Natural History Museum in Kensington.

www.sciencemuseum.org.uk
All about Kensington's Science Museum.

www.thebritishmuseum.ac.uk
A selection of the British Museum's collection of world cultural artefacts can be examined via the Compass online database of 3,000 items. ⓕ

www.vam.ac.uk
The world's largest decorative arts museum, the Victoria and Albert Museum is home to 145 galleries.

Regional
www.ashmol.ox.ac.uk
Ashmolean Museum of Art and Archaeology, Oxford.

www.english-heritage.org.uk
Links to historic buildings, landscapes and archaeological sites.

www.fitzmuseum.cam.ac.uk
Web home of Cambridge's Fitzwilliam Museum.

www.nmpft.org.uk
The National Museum of photography, film and television in Bradford.

UNITED STATES
General information
www.icom.org/vlmp/usa.html
Huge list of links to over 1,000 museums in the US.

www.museumstuff.com
Useful searchable directory of museum-related sites.

www.nationaltrust.org
The National Trust for Historic Preservation.

INTERNATIONAL ART GALLERIES AND MUSEUMS

This section contains a selection of sites from significant art galleries and museums around the world.

Austria

www.khm.at
Kunsthistorisches Museum, Vienna.

Belgium

www.fine-arts-museum.be
The Royal Museums of Fine Arts, Brussels.

Denmark

www.louisiana.dk
The Louisiana Museum of Modern Art, Humlebaek.

Finland

www.fng.fi
Finnish National Gallery.

www.kiasma.fi
Museum of Contemporary Art, Helsinki.

France

www.centrepompidou.fr
Pompidou Centre, aka the Beaubourg, Paris, one of Europe's premier arts centres, includes important temporary exhibitions and a significant permanent collection.

www.louvre.fr
The Louvre, Paris, one of the world's biggest museums of art. **Ⓕ**

www.musee-orsay.fr
The Musée d'Orsay, Paris, boasts a significant collection of Impressionist paintings.

Germany
www.smb.spk-berlin.de/ang
The Old National Gallery, Berlin.

Italy
www.uffizi.firenze.it
The Uffizi, Florence, the original gallery.

Japan
www.momak.go.jp
National Museum of Modern Art, Kyoto.

www.momat.go.jp
National Museum of Modern Art, Tokyo.

www.nmwa.go.jp
National Museum of Western Art, Tokyo.

www.tnm.go.jp
Tokyo National Museum.

Korea
www.metro.seoul.kr
Seoul Metropolitan Museum of Art.

www.moca.go.kr
Museum of Contemporary Art, Seoul.

Netherlands
www.amsterdammuseums.nl
Guide to 32 Amsterdam museums.

www.rijksmuseum.nl
The Rijksmuseum, Amsterdam, home to Rembrandt's *The Nightwatch*.

www.stedelijk.nl
Stedelijk Museum of Modern Art, Amsterdam.

www.vangoghmuseum.nl
Huge collection of post-Impressionist paintings at the Van Gogh Museum, Amsterdam.

Russia

www.hermitagemuseum.org
The splendid State Hermitage Museum of St Petersburg.🅕

www.museum.ru
Guide to the Museums of Russia.

www.museum.ru/gmii
The Pushkin Museum of Fine Arts, Moscow.

Spain

museoprado.mcu.es
Prado Museum, Madrid, home to a fine collection of Goya's works.

www.guggenheim-bilbao.es
Frank Gehry's postmodern architectural masterpiece, the Guggenheim Museum, Bilbao.

www.museothyssen.org
Thyssen-Bornemisza Museum, Madrid.

Sweden

www.modernamuseet.se
Modern Museum, Stockholm.

www.nationalmuseum.se
The National Museum, Stockholm.

ARCHITECTURE

Historically a branch of the fine arts, architecture is back on the agenda as a major subject for debate, as computer technology pushes the boundaries of postmodern construction techniques.

architronic.saed.kent.edu
Accessible archived 1992–97 issues of the scholarly architectural online journal *Architronic*.

cca.qc.ca
Montreal's Canadian Centre for Architecture, a museum and study centre devoted to international architecture.

www.architecture.com
Royal Institute of British Architects.

www.civictrust.org.uk
Founded to foster high standards of planning and architecture in towns and cities against the background of bomb damage and shoddy post-war development, the UK's Civic Trust charity aims to improve the places where people live and work.

www.greatbuildings.com
Thousands of buildings and hundreds of architects are documented at this gateway to architecture across the world, which includes many digital 3D models.**ᖴ**

www.jkl.fi/aalto
Museum, archives and academy of the important Finnish architect Alvar Aalto.

www.nbm.org
Washington DC's National Building Museum.

www.skyscrapernews.co.uk
The UK's tallest buildings under the spotlight: phantom and proposed projects, and buildings under construction.

www.skyscraperpage.com
This Vancouver-based site hosts the ultimate Worlds Tallest Building Diagram, photos and discussion forums about the world's tallest buildings.**⊕**

CULTURE

Culture with a big 'C' in this context can be taken to mean Websites that address a broad mix of popular and alternative culture and the arts. The postmodern approach.

www.culturevulture.net
Eclectic cultural links.

www.gazetteofthearts.com
Dense compendium of offbeat art links.**⊕**

www.plastic.com/altculture
Rock stars sit aside artists sit next to fizzy drinks in this alternative culture encyclopaedia.

DANCE
News and information
www.ballet.co.uk
Lots of information at this general dance overview site covering dance in the UK, with reviews, news and listings. Includes information about the Royal Ballet.

www.dancemagazine.com
Online site of the US dance mag.

www.londondance.com
Well designed dance portal with a directory of UK-based companies from London Arts and Sadler's Wells.**⊕**

www.sadlers-wells.com
Historical venue for dance, opera and music theatre.

www.sapphireswan.com/dance
Dance directory, with links ordered by dance type.

www.surrey.ac.uk/NRCD
UK National Resource Centre for Dance is an archive and
reference collection for the study of dance.

www.voiceofdance.com
US dance information site.

Ballet

Here's a selection of ballet company Websites.

www.abt.org
American Ballet Theatre.

www.alincom.com/bolshoi
Russia's Bolshoi Ballet.

www.atlantaballet.com
Atlanta Ballet.

www.ballet.org.uk
English National Ballet.

www.bostonballet.org
Boston Ballet.

www.houstonballet.org
Houston Ballet.

www.national.ballet.ca
The National Ballet of Canada.

www.nycballet.com
The New York City Ballet.

www.rambert.org.uk
Rambert Dance Company.

www.sfballet.org
San Francisco Ballet.

Modern and contemporary dance

GENERAL INFORMATION

www.cyberdance.org
Comprehensive classical and modern dance links site.

www.danceonline.com
Reviews, news and photography for dance around the world.

COMPANIES

www.amp.uk.com
Adventures in Motion Pictures.

www.dv8.co.uk
dv8 Physical Theatre.

www.markbaldwindance.com
Mark Baldwin Dance Company.

www.merce.org
Merce Cunningham Dance Company.**ⓕ**

www.ptdc.org
Paul Taylor Dance Company.

www.randomdance.org
Random Dance Company.

www.sddc.org.uk
Siobhan Davies Dance Company.

www.shobanajeyasingh.co.uk
Contemporary Indian dance with the Shobana Jeyasingh Dance Company.

www.theplace.org.uk
International centre for contemporary dance in London and home of the Richard Alston Dance Company.

LITERATURE

Literature is alive and well and on the Web. The Internet is frequently cited in some quarters as being responsible for a decline in literacy and reading. The evidence, however, suggests otherwise, with the Web opening up new readerships for classic texts, many of which are accessible for free. The Web literary scene itself also appears to be flourishing, with established poetry sites and salon-type journals finding healthy numbers of readers.

General information
books.guardian.co.uk
Literary review pages from the UK's most popular newspaper site.

www.pantheon.org/mythica.html
Reference site providing the background to myths and legends.

Literary and cultural commentary
Provocative, well written digital e-zines with attitude are one of the phenomena of the Web. They are often heavily text-based and feel all the better for it, providing an escape from the overload of images and animations that can interfere with the Web-reading experience. Providing intelligent debate, encompassing opinions and commentary on the arts, culture and politics, these sites are well worth perusing.

artsjournal.com
A daily digest of arts and cultural journalism.

slate.msn.com
News, politics and cultural commentary.

www.aldaily.com
Arts and Letters Daily, a compendium of ideas, criticism and

debate about the arts, ideas, trends and philosophy, drawn from a wide rage of Internet sources.

www.complete-review.com
Lively literary reviews and commentary. Well worth a read.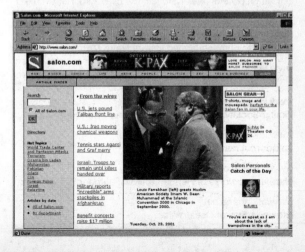

www.edge.org
Intellectual, philosophical, artistic and literary enquiry and debate.

www.eurozine.com
Communication and debate about the pressing issues of our time in four languages.

www.lrb.co.uk
London Review of Books, online edition.

www.prospect-magazine.co.uk
Political, intellectual and cultural debate in a selection of articles from recent editions of UK-based magazine *Prospect*.

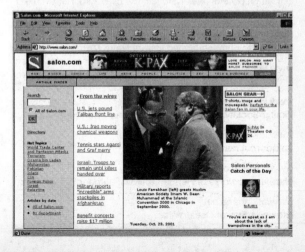

www.salon.com
Highly readable provocations and observations from US
Webzine Salon, with intriguing audio downloads of writers
and performers.**ⓕ**

www.villagevoice.com
Co-founded by Norman Mailer in 1955, New York's influential
alternative newspaper.

Links: News/Alternative News and Views

Authors

Many authors, both living and long gone, have Websites
dedicated to them.

martinamis.albion.edu
The Martin Amis Web.

www.cmgww.com/historic/kerouac
Official Website of Jack Kerouac, the beat author of *On the
Road*.

www.haroldpinter.org
Official site of much-lauded literary figure.**ⓕ**

www.jeanettewinterson.co.uk
Flashy site from the author of *Oranges Are Not the Only Fruit*.

www.kipling.org.uk
Kipling Society.

www.lewiscarroll.org/carroll.html
Author of *Alice in Wonderland*.

www.melville.org
The life and works of Herman Melville, author of *Moby-Dick*.

www.oscariana.net
Life and times of Oscar Wilde.

www.robertburns.org
The complete texts in several languages of the works of
Scotland's national poet, plus the full text of the Burns
Encyclopedia and details of the Burns House Museum.

www.showgate.com/tots/gross/wildeweb.html
We had to include this on the basis of its title alone – the
world wide Wilde web.

SHAKESPEARE
ipl.sils.umich.edu/reading/shakespeare/shakespeare.html
Shakespeare's texts courtesy of the Internet Public Library
and Bartleby.com.

www.chemicool.com/Shakespeare
Another route to the *Complete Works*.

www.shakespeare.org.uk
The Shakespeare Birthplace Trust, Stratford-upon-Avon, UK.

Online texts
classics.mit.edu
Over 400 works of classical literature for free at the Internet
Classics Archive.

www.bartleby.com
Excellent site providing literature, reference and verse texts
free of charge. **F**

www.bibliomania.com
Impressive site providing free access to over 2,000 texts,
study guides and reference resources. **F**

Poetry
shoga.wwa.com/%7Ergs/glossary.html
Useful glossary of poetic terms.

wings.buffalo.edu/epc
Electronic Poetry Center.

www.dialoguepoetry.org
Building a culture of peace and non-violence through
poetry.❻

www.poems.com
A new poem every day at Poetry Daily.

www.poetry.nl
Poetry International, Rotterdam, Netherlands.

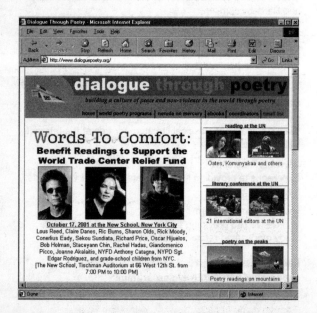

www.poets.org
The Academy of American Poets.

www.ubu.com
Visual, Concrete and Sound Poetry.

Literary museums
www.bronte.org.uk
Brontë Parsonage Museum, Haworth, West Yorkshire, UK.

www.dickensmuseum.com
The Dickens House Museum, London, UK.

www.strindbergsmuseet.se
August Strindberg Museum, Stockholm, Sweden.

THEATRE
Websites are an important device for reaching potential theatre audiences, and there is an abundance of theatre listing and review sites. Many of these provide online ticketing facilities which enable purchasers to select seats.

General
www.theatre-link.com
Copious links to theatre sites.

National
United Kingdom

Listings and tickets
www.albemarle-london.com
West End theatre guide.

www.londonnet.co.uk/ln/out/ent/theatre.html
London Net's theatre guide.

www.officiallondontheatre.co.uk
Theatre guide from the Society of London Theatre.

www.theatrenow.com
News, features and comment on all the latest London openings and events.

www.uktw.co.uk
The UK Theatre Web includes online ticket booking facilities.

www.whatsonstage.com
West End theatre news and tickets.

London theatres
www.donmar-warehouse.com
The Donmar Warehouse, in the heart of Soho.

www.nationaltheatre.org.uk
The National Theatre Online.

www.royalcourttheatre.com
Royal Court Theatre.

www.rsc.org.uk
Official Royal Shakespeare Company Website.

www.shakespeares-globe.org
Shakespeare's Globe Theatre, Bankside, London.

Other
www.thestage.co.uk
Online version of well established UK newspaper which includes theatre reviews, news and auditions.**F**

UNITED STATES
Listings and tickets
www.americantickets.com
New York theatre and sporting events tickets.

www.americantheaterweb.com
News and listings for theatre across the US.

www.broadway.com
Headlines and tickets.

www.broadwaytheater.com
Broadway reviews and tickets.

www.playbill.com
Broadway theatre information.

www.theatermania.com
Nationwide listings and news.

Other
www.broadwaystars.com
Collected links to newspaper reviews and columns, plus news.

www.ibdb.com
The Internet Broadway Database maintains records of productions since the beginning of Broadway theatre.

www.nytheatre.com
The New York Theatre Experience.

www.talkinbroadway.com
Broadway and off-Broadway discussion, information and reviews, incorporating the Internet Theatre Database.❻

www.variety.com
Online version of the entertainment publication that has provided news and analysis since 1905.

Links: Film and the Movies
        Music
        Radio and Television

Astrology

Few of us can say that we haven't occasionally been interested to hear what the stars have to say. Horoscopes continue to hold an unshakeable fascination and this is reflected in the huge numbers of star sign readings found on the Web. They are particularly prevalent as pages in magazine-style sites which often reflect the content of their printed counterparts. However, there's much more to astrology than horoscopes, and there are plenty of sites which explore the more diverse methods of reading the present and the future, including Chinese and Indian astrology, and lunar readings.

hinduastrology.com
Indian astrological services via a site that proves difficult to navigate.

thenewage.com
Astrology software packages for 'beginners, professionals and entrepreneurs' from Matrix software. Plus personal reports for the 'astrologically curious'. As you may be able to foretell, these don't come free.

www.astroadvice.com
Astrology readings, with tarot, palmistry and AstroBingo all thrown in for good measure.

www.astro-fengshui.com
Combined Chinese astrology and feng shui site, with the emphasis on the latter.

www.astrologer.com
The Metalog resource on this UK site offers directory links to professional counselling astrologers. Also home to the Astrological Association of Great Britain.

www.astrology.com
Part of the ivillage.com women's network.

www.astrologyalive.com
Straight and to the point monthly horoscopes.

www.astrologycom.com
Detailed site from Australia run by an 'A-Team' of six.

www.astrologyguide.com
Basic site from the About.com network.

www.astrologyindex.com
Daily horoscopes by e-mail, plus astrology charts and sign compatibility.

www.astrologyinsights.com
Attractive site with 'Ask Ruby' personal advice column.**ⓕ**

www.astrology-online.com
Lots of typefaces on this independent site.

www.astrosonia.com
Chinese astrology from amateur Sonia. Beware of the pop-up ads.

www.astrospeak.com
Predictions from an Indian perspective. Instant astrology, tarot and numerology readings.

www.chinese-astrology.com
Entertaining site where you can find out which animal sign you are. Includes a Hall of Shame which names and shames other sites that have recycled material from this site.

www.easyscopes.com
It doesn't come any easier than this link site: receive your horoscope in Dutch, English, French or German from a variety of different astrologers.

www.femail.co.uk/pages/horoscopes
Sun and Moon readings from Associated New Media's women's site.

www.journalofastrology.com
Website of the Vedic *Journal of Astrology*.

www.live-astro.com/horoscopes
Standard horoscopes, plus live audioscopes with Russell Grant.

www.starlightastrology.com
Daily, weekly and monthly horoscopes with optional custom birth charts.

Country Information

This section concentrates on regional information about boundary-defined areas, such as continents, countries and states. This should be distinguished from the travel-related country information that can be found in the Travel section.

GENERAL

The sites below provide demographical, geographical, statistical and other such factual information for countries and regions around the world.

www.emulateme.com
Aiming to 'eradicate conflict by increasing cultural awareness', this site provides basic information about the economy, defence, geography, government and people of the countries of the world, from Afghanistan to Zimbabwe. National flags and cheesy midi-renditions of national anthems also provided.

www.insideworld.com
An excellent network of country portals, news services and country information can be reached via this central news portal, plus free daily newsletters on selected countries.**F**

www.internets.com/scountry.htm
Links to country and regional Websites.

www.nationsonline.org
Useful links for both country and travel information.

www.odci.gov/cia/publications/factbook
The CIA *World Factbook* from the US.

www.your-nation.com
Country comparisons and rankings based on the CIA *Factbook*.

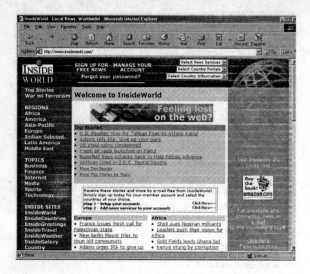

REGIONAL AND NATIONAL SEARCH ENGINES AND DIRECTORIES

These sites provide searchable links and routes to local information, such as social services, businesses and commercial outlets for specific countries, regions, cities and towns.

Australia

askjeeves.com.au
au.altavista.com
au.yahoo.com
ninemsn.com.au
www.aaa.com.au
www.aboriginalaustralia.com
www.anzwers.com.au

www.citysearch.com.au
www.goeureka.com.au
www.netguide.com.au
www.ozsearch.com.au
www.sofcom.com.au/Directories
www.vicnet.net.au
www.webwombat.com.au
www.yourguide.com.au/yourguide.asp

Canada

ca.msn.com
ca.yahoo.com
canadopedia.com
cantrek.com
portal.tc.ca
webcity.ca.iscapenetwork.com
www.ab.sympatico.ca
www.aboriginalcanada.gc.ca
www.alcanseek.com
www.canada.com
www.canadiancontent.net
www.canadianeh.com
www.canadaseek.com
www.canoe.ca
www.searchcanada.com
www.windfall.ca

New Zealand

netguide.co.nz
nz.altavista.com
nzcity.co.nz
nzexplorer.co.nz
nzoom.com
www.accessnz.co.nz

www.enzed.com
www.newzealand.co.nz
www.newzealandnz.co.nz
www.nzpages.co.nz
www.nzsearch.co.nz
www.piperpat.co.nz
www.searchnz.co.nz
www.tourism.net.nz

South Africa

Many of these sites cover Africa, the continent, as well as South Africa, the country.

sa.web-chart.com
www.ananzi.co.za
www.dailyafrican.com
www.goafrica.co.za
www.msn.co.za
www.mweb.co.za
www.saeverything.co.za
www.southafrica.co.za
www.woyaa.com

United Kingdom

uk.altavista.com
uk.searchengine.com
uk.yahoo.com
www.250000.co.uk
www.ask.co.uk
www.cyberbritain.com
www.dotfamilies.co.uk
www.great-british-pages.co.uk
www.hermia.com
www.msn.co.uk
www.scoot.co.uk

www.scotland247.co.uk
www.uk250.co.uk
www.ukfavourites.com
www.ukindex.co.uk
www.uknetguide.co.uk
www.ukplanet.com
www.ukplus.com
www.upmystreet.com

United States

www.altavista.com
www.aol.com
www.asianindiansinusa.com
www.askjeeves.com
www.blackwebportal.com
www.digital-neighbors.com
www.indians.org
www.msn.com
www.musalman.com
www.town-usa.com
www.wafin.com
www.yahoo.com

Other country and regional portals

almashriq.hiof.no
Directory of Middle East links.

english.ajeeb.com
Middle East portal in English.

www.123india.com
Directory for India.

www.afrika.no/index
The Index on Africa, with nearly 2,000 links, is maintained by the Norwegian Council for Africa.

www.arabia.com/english
Considered by many to be the leading Arab world Internet site.

www.euroseek.com
European searches in many languages.

www.indiatimes.com
Directory site from the *Times of India*.

www.kamat.com
Independent and idiosyncratic, Kamat's Potpourri entertainingly
examines the history, divinity and diversity of India.

www.orientation.com
Search directories for regions across the world, including
Asia, central and eastern Europe and Latin America.**ⓕ**

www.ru
The shortest of addresses for one of the largest of countries.
The Russia on the Net directory has been online since 1995.

www.search.ch
Swiss search engine.

www.searcheurope.com
Directory for Europe.

www.searchindia.com
India directory.

www.searchmalta.com
Information about Malta.

www.yandex.ru/index_engl.html
Alternative search engine for Russia.

Links: Genealogy/National Archives
       Travel/National Travel Portals
       Travel/Travel Resources
       Maps/National Street and Location Maps

Education, Reference and Research

The sites listed here are concerned with structured learning and knowledge, including adult and child education sites, dictionaries and other sites exploring the English language, languages and language learning, plus a selection of academic research sites and libraries.

Packed as it is with masses of information, there's a strong argument that the Internet is the world's biggest encyclopaedia in its own right, with search engines being the means of sorting and presenting information in advanced ways to allow access to the huge unstructured reservoir of information. Under the Encyclopaedias heading below are listed sites that use more conventional means of encompassing and subdividing the whole of human knowledge.

EDUCATION

www.bigchalk.com
US national education portal.

www.edufind.com
Worldwide educational institution locator.

www.gcse.com
Tutorials, tips and advice on UK GCSE coursework and exams.

www.hotcourses.com
Large selection of UK colleges and course givers.

www.learndirect.co.uk
UK government's online vocational courses search facility.

www.lifelonglearning.co.uk
Government site encouraging, promoting and developing lifelong learning.

www.naso.org.uk
Lifelong learning may be the latest educational buzz-phrase, but the UK National Adult School Union has had that objective for the last 200 years.

www.nec.ac.uk
The UK National Extension College, widening access to education for adults through distance learning.

www.ngfl.gov.uk
Government-sponsored UK National Grid For Learning link site to education and lifelong learning resources and information.

www.niace.org.uk
The UK National Organisation for Adult Learning.

www.oca-uk.com
The UK Open College of the Arts encourages creative personal expression.

www.open.ac.uk
Established in 1971, the Open University is the UK's largest university and provides courses throughout the world.

www.wea.org.uk
The Worker's Educational Association is the UK's largest voluntary provider of adult learning opportunities.

Links: Kids

Online learning
elearners.com
US-based directory of online distance learning courses and degrees.

www.fathom.com
Knowledge trails provide a different approach to education at this interesting online course site provided by a coalition of universities and museums.**F**

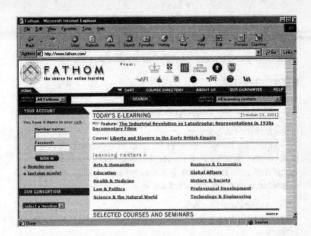

REFERENCE

General reference

beta.encarta.msn.com
Encarta, from Microsoft, includes an online encyclopaedia, dictionary, atlas and the Enquire integrated search facility.

www.findarticles.com
A vast archive of published articles dating back to 1998 from more than 300 magazines and journals searchable for free.

www.ibiblio.org
Publicly-maintained collection of searchable collated information.

www.infoplease.com
US education resource combining encyclopaedia, dictionary, atlas and almanacs loaded with statistics, facts, and historical records.

www.xrefer.com
Billed as 'the web's first reference engine', xrefer cross-references encyclopaedias, dictionaries, thesauri and books of quotations from the world's leading publishers.🄵

ENCYCLOPAEDIAS
www.bartleby.com/65
The US *Columbia Encyclopedia* online.

www.britannica.com
The standard encyclopaedia for over 200 years, this is a search and directory site incorporating sections of the *Encyclopaedia Britannica*. A premium subscription service is available which provides full access.

www.encyclopedia.com
With over 50,000 articles and additional links to the Electric Library.

WORLD TIME
Local times around the world:
www.hilink.com.au/times
www.humanclock.com🄵
www.timeticker.com
www.worldtime.com

Language

DICTIONARIES
dictionary.cambridge.org
Cambridge Dictionaries Online.

www.m-w.com
Merriam-Webster English-American dictionary.

www.wordsmyth.net
Wordsmyth, the educational dictionary-thesaurus.

www.yourdictionary.com
Huge collection of indexed links to 1,800 dictionaries, including specialised subjects and 260 different languages. **F**

LANGUAGE USE AND WRITERS' AIDS

humanities.uchicago.edu/forms_unrest/ROGET.html
University-uploaded version of *Roget's Thesaurus*, online and searchable.

phrases.shu.ac.uk
Phrases, sayings and clichés at The Phase Finder, with explanations of meaning and origins.

rhyme.lycos.com
RhymeZone rhyming dictionary and thesaurus.

www.acronymfinder.com
Over 200,000 defined acronyms and abbreviations.

www.ag.wastholm.net
Brush up your wit at Aphorisms Galore!

www.atomiser.demon.co.uk/abbrev
Discover the meaning of those TLAs with The Great Letter Abbreviation Hunt.

www.cogsci.princeton.edu/~wn
WordNet, a lexical database for the English language from Princeton University.

www.quotegallery.com
Quotes searchable by author, by category and alphabetically.

www.thesaurus.com
Searchable thesaurus and dictionary combined.

www.westegg.com/cliche
Nearly 3,500 indexed US clichés.

www.word2word.com/alphabet.html
Alphabets of the World.

www.wordexplorations.com
Check the Resources Dictionary here for interesting and exciting links to word-oriented sites, including Oxymora lists and educational links.

www.wordlab.com
Playing with words.

www.wordorigins.org
Origins of selected words and phrases.

SLANG AND COLLOQUIALISM

odps.cyberscriber.com
The Online Dictionary of Playground Slang has phrases mainly of British origins, but welcomes contributions from countries with English as a first language.

www.chemistry.co.nz/kiwi.htm
New Zealand words and phrases.

www.londonslang.com
Rhyming slang and Estuary English.

www.peevish.co.uk/slang
UK slang and colloquialisms.

www.word2word.com/slang.html
Links to slang and cussing sites, including Aussie slang and sayings page.

Languages

MULTILINGUAL TRANSLATION DICTIONARIES

dictionaries.travlang.com
Language dictionaries for travellers.

dictionary.ajeeb.com/en.htm
Arabic – English – French – German – Turkish.

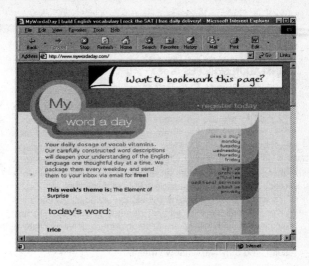

nz.com/NZ/Culture/NZDic.html
New Zealand English to US English Dictionary.

www.ectaco.com
Electronic translation dictionary across many languages.

www.foreignword.com
Language portal accessing over 300 online translation
dictionaries.

www.get-together.net
Another manifestation of the ectaco dictionary.

www.langtolang.com
Word translation across seven languages.

www.leo.org/~mike/dictionaries.html
Huge collection of links to translation dictionaries.

www.mywordaday.com
Build your knowledge of English day-by-day with single word definitions sent by e-mail. ❻

TRANSLATION SERVICES

Machine translation

These services provide translation by computer and are designed to provide an instantaneous summary of meaning, rather than exact and accurate translations, which would take much longer to achieve. Most of the machine translation services are free and some sites also offer cost upgrades to a higher level of translation via either a human translator on a project basis, or downloadable software packages.

It's worth testing machine translation services, as each will deliver translations with varying degrees of success. To say they are not infallible is an understatement. If you create a paragraph, copy and paste it into each, and compare the results, you may see what we mean.

babelfish.altavista.com
Named after the *Hitch-hiker's Guide*'s own translation resource.

websmart.kielikone.fi
English-Finnish translations.

www.alis.com/translate_online.html
Gist-In-Time is quick and simple to use.

www.alphaworks.ibm.com/aw.nsf/html/mt
This has one of the cleanest interfaces, but in our admittedly limited test, it churned out badly mangled Franglais.

www.foreignword.com/Tools/transnow.htm
Access to 22 different machine translation systems from this one central point, plus free downloadable translation tool. ❻

www.freetranslation.com
Quick and clean, this service from SDL seems to offer a high level of translation.

www.reverso.net/textonly
Usefully shows translation side-by-side with the original text.

www.t-mail.com
Free e-mail and Webpage translation service.**❻**

Other machine translation services

www.systransoft.com
www.tranexp.com:2000
www.worldlingo.com

Other translation services

www.amikai.com
Web, e-mail, chat and text translation services.

www.babylon.com
Babylon-pro is a translation, information and conversion tool. Free trial copies are available.

LANGUAGE LEARNING

In addition to the following sites, many of the translation dictionaries above also provide language learning facilities.

www.bbc.co.uk/education/languages
BBC Online's language learning site.

www.elanguage.com/eng/reference/dictionary.asp
Hear how words are pronounced with this excellent talking dictionary.**❻**

www.sil.org
SIL International has studied, developed and documented the world's lesser known languages for over 50 years.

www.travlang.com
A confusing home page at this language learning resource site.

RESEARCH
Research sites
One of the earliest uses of the Internet and the origin of the Web was as a means of pooling and sharing academic and research information and resources. It's no surprise therefore that there is a huge amount of research information available via innumerable Websites, including millions of articles and research papers. In many ways the academic research sites form a separate world within the Web. Below are listed just a few of the many thousands of Websites that cater to the research community.

biome.ac.uk
Hub for Internet resources in the health and life sciences.

plato.stanford.edu/contents.html
Stanford Encyclopedia of Philosophy, free and searchable.

uncweb.carl.org
Ingenta is the world's largest Website for the search and delivery of research articles, searching nearly 3 million articles from over 25,000 publications.

www.anthro.net
Links and references for anthropology, archaeology, history, linguistics, psychology, sociology and other social sciences.

www.biography.com
25,000 quick and concise biographical details, past and present.

www.boxmind.com
Excellent resource for research, with a great design. Optional access to an online video lecture series.**F**

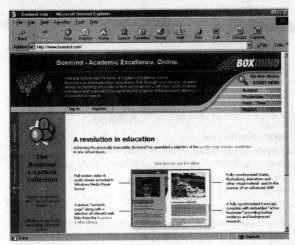

www.data-archive.ac.uk
Specialist national resource containing the largest collection of accessible computer readable data in the social sciences and humanities in the United Kingdom.

www.h-net.msu.edu
H-Net creates and coordinates discussion networks, and sponsors over 100 free scholar-edited newsletters, relating to the arts, social sciences and humanities.

www.humbul.ac.uk
Online Humanities resources.

www.liv.ac.uk/Philosophy/philos.html
Liverpool University's Philosophy at Large portal.

www.northernlight.com
The Special Collection of over 7,000 full text publications is particularly useful at this respected search engine.

www.philosophers.co.uk
Online version of *The Philosopher's Magazine* from the UK.

www.philosophy-forum.org
The Forum for European Philosophy aims at encouraging communication between academic philosophers and the wider public.

www.philosophynow.demon.co.uk
Online version of UK philosophy magazine.

www.psigate.ac.uk
Access to high quality Internet-based resources in the physical sciences: astronomy, chemistry, earth sciences, physics, science history and policy, and aspects of the material sciences.

www.radicalphilosophy.com
UK journal of socialist and feminist philosophy, founded in 1972.

www.rdn.ac.uk
Service aiming to provide access to high quality Internet resources for the learning, teaching and research community. Other users may also find the service to be of value for personal and professional development.

www.regard.ac.uk
Database service for social science research funded by the UK Economic and Social Research Council, with over 65,000 records dating back to the mid-80s.

www.searchedu.com
Claims to search over 15 million university and education Webpages.

www.sociology.org
Non-commercial *Electronic Journal of Sociology*.

www.socresonline.org.uk
Sociological Research Online.

www.sosig.ac.uk
The Social Science Information Gateway (SOSIG) aims to provide a trusted source of selected, high quality Internet information for researchers and practitioners in the social sciences, business and law. It is part of the UK Resource Discovery Network.

www.utm.edu/research/iep
The Internet Encyclopedia of Philosophy.

Libraries

As more searchable catalogues come online, library Websites provide invaluable research facilities.

sunsite.berkeley.edu/Libweb
Excellent worldwide library link site.**❻**

www.ifla.org
International Association of Library Associations and Institutions.

NATIONAL LIBRARIES
aleph.salib.ac.za
The National Library of South Africa.

www.bl.uk
The British Library.

www.bodley.ox.ac.uk
The Bodleian Library, Oxford University.

www.bpl.org
The Boston Public Library.

www.folusa.com
Friends of Libraries USA.

www.huntington.org/LibraryDiv/LibraryHome.html
The Huntington Library, California.

www.lcweb.loc.gov
US Library of Congress.

www.morganlibrary.org
The Pierpont Morgan Library, Museum and Research Library,
New York.

www.natlib.govt.nz
The National Library of New Zealand.

www.nla.gov.au
The National Library of Australia.

www.nlc-bnc.ca
The National Library of Canada.

www.nypl.org
The New York Public Library.

ONLINE LIBRARIES
ask.elibrary.com
www.ibiblio.org
www.vlib.org

Links: Genealogy/National Archives
Country Information
Part One/Searching the Net

Environmental Issues and World Concerns

This section deals with those often hidden issues and subject areas that the Net has brought into the public domain. These are generally not part of the mainstream flow of media information, which is increasingly controlled by corporate interests.

The Net is often proclaimed as one of the great democratising forces, and it's certainly true that it has made possible an unprecedented degree of sharing of information between groups of people across geographical boundaries and over great distances. In addition to linking groups with a common interest, Websites have provided the public with easily accessible information about these groups' activities.

Not-for-profit and charity organisations find the Net a highly effective way of communicating both internally and with each other, and a useful means of making publicly available information relating to human rights, disaster and poverty relief, freedom of speech, the impacts of globalisation, and environmental and wildlife protection, for example, in a way that has not previously been possible.

GENERAL

netaction.org
Promoting the Internet for effective grassroots citizen action.

www.apc.org
The Association for Progressive Communications, advocating the use of the Internet for promoting environmental, human rights, development and peace issues.**❻**

www.geocities.com/CapitolHill/Lobby/4192
A one-stop link site to the Leftist Parties of the World.

www.gn.apc.org
Network support for groups and individuals working for the environment, development, peace and human rights.**❻**

www.igc.org/igc/gateway/index.html
The Internet's Progressive Gateway from the Institute
for Global Communications, which works to facilitate
networking and collaboration towards the aim of a healthier
society. Hosts PeaceNet, EcoNet, WomensNet and
AntiRacismNet. ❻

www.imf.org
The International Monetary Fund.

www.love-or-money.org
Asking all those difficult questions ...

www.neravt.com/left
Leftist and Progressive Internet Resources Directory.

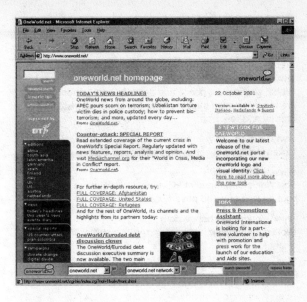

www.oneworld.net

OneWorld is a community of over 950 organisations working for social justice. **ᴳ**

www.panos.org.uk

International institute providing information and stimulating debate on global issues with a developing country perspective.

www.protest.net

Collective of activists working to create an alternative media. Includes a calendar of protest, meetings and conferences.

www.tides.org
Body supporting positive social change which provides
funding for progressive community-based non-profit
organisations.

www.tni.org
Global economics, peace and security, and democratisation
are the three main thrusts of the Transnational Institute's
activity and research.

www.unesco.org
United Nations Educational, Scientific and Cultural Organisation.

www.wdm.org.uk
The World Development Movement, tackling the underlying
root causes of world poverty. ❻

www.workingforchange.com
Working, shopping, volunteering, giving and acting for social
change.

www.worldbank.org
The World Bank Group.

AIDS

app.netaid.org/programs/HIV
An overview of the fight against AIDS from NetAid.org.

nzaf.org.nz
The New Zealand AIDS Foundation.

www.aids.org.za
The AIDS Foundation of South Africa.

www.aegis.com
The Aids Information Global Education System. ❻

www.redribbon.co.za
Information site about the spread of AIDS in Africa.

www.tht.org.uk
The Terence Higgins Trust, the largest UK AIDS and HIV charity.

Links: Health

ANIMAL RIGHTS

www.peta-online.org
People for the Ethical Treatment of Animals.

Links: Nature/Animal Protection Agencies

CHILD PROTECTION AND RIGHTS

www.childline.co.uk
Website of the UK's 24-hour helpline for children and young
people in trouble or danger.

www.cpag.org.uk
The Child Poverty Action Group has been fighting poverty in
the UK for more than 30 years.

www.crin.org
Children's Rights Information Network disseminates
information about the rights of children to its membership of
more than 1,100 organisations in over 100 countries.

www.efcw.org
The European Forum for Child Welfare provides information
to its members throughout Europe.

www.ifcw.org
The International Forum for Child Welfare.

www.ridbc.org.au
Australian Royal Institute for Deaf and Blind Children.

www.savethechildren.org.uk
The UK's leading international children's charity works in 70
countries.

www.sids.org.uk
Foundation for the Study of Infant Deaths, the UK's leading cot death charity.

www.the-childrens-society.org.uk
UK charity working to uphold children's rights.

www.unicef.org
The United Nations Children's Fund.

CONFLICT, DISASTER AND POVERTY RELIEF

www.actionaid.org
Working in over 30 countries to relieve poverty.

www.alertnet.org
AlertNet from the Reuters Foundation provides global news, communications and logistics services to the international disaster relief community and the public. 🄵

www.cafod.org.uk
The Catholic Agency For Overseas Development.

www.christian-aid.org.uk
An agency of the churches in the UK and Ireland working through local organisations to relieve poverty regardless of religious beliefs.

www.crisisweb.org
Influential organisation committed to strengthening the capacity of the international community to anticipate, understand and act to prevent and contain conflict. 🄵

www.ifrc.org
Disaster response and preparedness, as well as the promotion of humanitarian values, community health and care are at the heart of the International Red Cross and Red Crescent Societies.

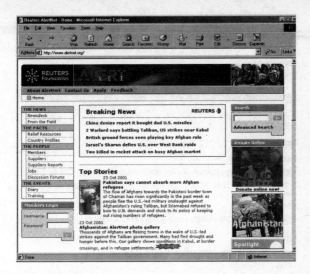

www.netaid.org
Through powerful public-private partnerships, and in alliance with Internet users, Netaid.org is aiming to create the largest global online community acting on extreme poverty worldwide.❻

www.oxfam.org.uk
The Oxford Committee for Famine Relief has come a long way since its creation in 1942 in response to the Nazi occupation of Greece. Oxfam is now established as one of the leading international development, relief and campaigning organisations tackling poverty worldwide.❻

www.reliefweb.int
Information for the relief community supplied by the UN.

www.wateraid.org.uk
Working to enable communities in Asia and Africa to provide
themselves with a safe water supply and adequate sanitation.

www.wfp.org
The United Nations' World Food Programme.

Links: Environmental Issues and World Concerns/Volunteering

DRUGS
International
www.atod.org
Virtual Clearing House on Alcohol, Tobacco and Other Drugs,
hosted by the Canadian Centre on Substance Abuse.

www.ihra.net
The International Harm Reduction Association.

www.incb.org
The International Narcotics Control Board.

By country

www.adf.org.au	Australia
www.ceida.net.au	Australia
www.chr.asn.au	Australia
www.fds.org.au	Australia
www.ccsa.ca	Canada
www.brugerforeningen.dk	Denmark
www.needle.co.nz	New Zealand
www.nzdf.org.nz	New Zealand
www.droleg.ch/e_index.html	Switzerland
www.ahrn.net	Thailand
www.cascade.u-net.com	United Kingdom
www.trashed.co.uk	United Kingdom
www.ukhra.org	United Kingdom
www.csdp.org	United States

www.drcnet.org	United States
www.droleg.ch	United States
www.drugsense.org	United States
www.health.org	United States
www.heroinhelper.com	United States
www.herointimes.com	United States

General information:

www.erowid.org
www.poppies.org

Links: Health and Medical

ELDERLY AND AGEING

eurolinkage.org
European network concerned with older people and the issues of ageing.

www.ageconcern.org.nz
Age Concern New Zealand.

www.ageconcern.org.uk
The leading charitable movement in the UK concerned with ageing and older people.

www.cpa.org.uk
UK Centre for Policy on Ageing.

www.helpage.org
Helpage International works with and for disadvantaged older people worldwide.❻

www.ifa-fiv.org
The International Federation on Ageing, a consultative organisation to the UN.

www.ilcuk.org.uk
The UK branch of the International Longevity Centre, an

independent think-tank concerned with research and policy on ageing and society.

www.ilcusa.org
US International Longevity Center.

www.qmuc.ac.uk/sshc/cenolder/links.htm
Link page to sites addressing issues relating to the elderly.

Links: Silver Surfers, Seniors, Over 50s

EUTHANASIA

www.euthanasia.com
US site providing information for research on euthanasia, physician-assisted suicide, living wills and mercy killing.

www.euthanasia.org
Exit's Fast Access resource for Euthanasia information at this UK site.

www.finalexit.org
The Euthanasia Research and Guidance Organization's World Directory.

www.hemlock.org
The US Hemlock Society.

www.iaetf.org
International Task Force on euthanasia and assisted suicide.

www.prolifeinfo.com/euthanasia.html
Euthanasia page from the Ultimate Pro-Life Resource List.

www.ves.org.uk
Established in 1935, the UK Voluntary Euthanasia Society was the first organisation of its type in the world.❻

ENVIRONMENT AND ECOLOGY

General environmental and ecological sites

forests.org
Worldwide conservation portal connecting to information about forests, rainforests and biodiversity.

wilderness.org.au
The Wilderness Society of Australia.

www.british-trees.com
Forestry conservation site, including Native British Tree Guide.

www.cat.org.uk
The Center for Alternative Technology explores sustainable solutions.

www.conservationfoundation.co.uk
Promoting and managing positive environmental projects.

www.cpre.org.uk
Council for the Protection of Rural England.

www.ea.gov.au
Australian government environmental site.

www.earthlife.org.za
Politics and the environment intertwined at this South African site.

www.earthtimes.org
Daily newspaper addressing the human environment and related economic, humanitarian and social issues.🄵

www.english-nature.org.uk
Government agency that champions the conservation of wildlife and natural features throughout England.

www.environment-agency.gov.uk
UK government Environment Agency.

www.environmentdaily.com
Environmental news service for Europe. **F**

www.foe.co.uk
Friends of the Earth UK.

www.foe.org
Friends of the Earth US.

www.fscoax.org
The Mexico-based Forest Stewardship Council works to ensure the environmentally appropriate, socially beneficial and economically viable management of the world's forests.

www.globalhemp.com
Portal to the hemp community.

www.greenhousenet.org
Global warming information.

www.greenpeace.org
The high profile environmental lobbying and action organisation is now over 30 years old and has offices in 39 countries, including

www.greenpeace.org.au	Australia
www.greenpeacecanada.org	Canada
www.greenpeace.org.nz	New Zealand
www.greenpeace.org.uk	United Kingdom
www.greenpeaceusa.org	United States

www.oss.org.uk
Founded in 1865, the Open Spaces Society is Britain's oldest conservation society and exists to protect common land and public rights of way.

www.rainforestfoundationuk.org
UK-based rainforest protection charity.

www.seafriends.org.nz
There's a huge amount of information at this New Zealand-based conservation site.

www.surfrider.org.au
Australian group seeking to protect the world's waves and beaches through conservation, activism, research and education.

www.sustlife.com
The Sustainable Life Portal links to environmental, ecological and organic resources.

www.theecologist.org
Online edition of *The Ecologist*, the world's longest running environmental magazine.

www.the-environment-council.org.uk
Independent UK environmental charity.

www.tidybritain.org.uk
Working for litter-free and sustainable environments.

www.unep.org
United Nations Environment Programme.

www.woodland-trust.org.uk
The Woodland Trust is the UK's leading conservation charity dedicated to the protection of our native woodland heritage.

www.wri.org/wri
The World Resources Institute provides information, ideas and solutions to global environmental problems.❺

Light pollution

www.dark-skies.freeserve.co.uk
www.darksky.org

The green movement

www.eco-web.com
The Global Directory for Environmental Technology.

www.forumforthefuture.org.uk
Influential organisation with sustainable development as its
objective.

www.globalactionplan.org.uk
How to go green at home.

www.greenfutures.org.uk
Website of UK environmental solutions magazine.

www.ihre.org

GREEN PARTY

www.greens.org.au	Australia
green.ca	Canada
www.tgouwp.edu/greens	India
www.degroenen.nl	Netherlands
www.greens.org.nz	New Zealand
www.greenparty.org.za	South Africa
www.greenparty.org.uk	United Kingdom
www.scottishgreens.org.uk	Scotland
www.greenparty.org	United States
www.europeangreens.org	Europe
www.greenparties.org	Worldwide
www.gruppom.com/gm	Worldwide

Waste and recycling

www.compost-uk.org.uk
Research and advice on composting as a sustainable
solution to organic waste management.

www.letsrecycle.com
Independent site providing recycling and waste management
information for the UK.

www.sas.org.uk
Surfers Against Sewage, a UK group fighting for a clean, safe water environment.**❺**

Other Waste and Recycling Sites

www.recycle-more.co.uk
www.tidybritain.org.uk
www.wastewatch.org.uk

FOOD PRODUCTION AND GM FOODS

www.animalfeed.org.uk
Campaigning against GM animal feed.

www.connectotel.com/gmfood
Indexed link site to world GM food news.

www.cropgen.org
Making the case for genetically modified foods, UK-based CropGen is funded by the crop biotechnology industry.

www.foodfuture.org.uk
GM debating forum from the UK's Food and Drink Federation.

www.geneticfoodalert.org.uk
Campaigning for a GM-free trade and a ban on the production, import and sale of GM foods and crops.

www.geneticsforum.org.uk
Independent UK organisation concerned with the use of new genetic technologies and their public policy implications.

www.msc.org
The Marine Stewardship Council promotes environmentally responsible stewardship of the world's most important renewable food source.

www.pure.food.org
The US Organics Consumers Association campaigns for food safety, organic agriculture, fair trade and sustainability.

Links: Food/Organic
Environmental Issues and World Concerns/Genetic Engineering

FREEDOM OF SPEECH AND CENSORSHIP

www.eff.org
Electronic Frontier Foundation, fighting to protect freedom of speech in a digital age. **Ⓕ**

www.freedomforum.org
US-based international forum dedicated to free press and free speech.

www.indexoncensorship.org
Website of the UK magazine which seeks to record abuses of free expression rights, as well as openly debate the issues of the day. This site also provides newslogs and discussion forums.**⑤**

www.openwords.com
Freedom of speech resources.

www.prwatch.org
Quarterly online newsletter about manipulative and misleading PR practices from the Center for Media and Democracy.

www.rsf.fr
Since 1985 Reporters Sans Frontières, or Reporters Without Borders, has supported press freedom worldwide.**⑤**

Links: News/Alternative News and Views

GENETIC ENGINEERING

www.gene-watch.org
The US Council for Responsible Genetics encourages informed public debate about the social, ethical and environmental implications of new genetic technologies.

www.genewatch.org
Independent organisation concerned with the ethics and risks of genetic engineering in a wider context.**⑤**

GLOBALISATION
Globalisation issues
www.fairtrade.org.uk
Trying to creating a fairer commercial world.

www.focusweb.org
Focusing on the Global South in a connected world.

www.ifg.org
The International Forum on Globalisation.

www.imf.org
The International Monetary Fund.

www.nologo.org
From the book of the same name.

www.oneworld.org/ni
New Internationalist magazine online.

www.unctad.org
United Nations Conference on Trade and Development.

www.wto.org
Swiss-based World Trade Organisation.

Activism, anti-capitalism and corporations

theyrule.orgo.org
They know who we are. Do we know who they are? Flash
route to corporate information.

www.adbusters.org
Undermining the commercial world.

www.corporatewatch.org.uk
Activism against corporate rule and influence through research.

www.corpwatch.org
US organisation that seeks to hold corporations accountable.

www.essential.org
Site with a mission to provide access to vital information to
grassroots organisations about subjects neglected by the
mass media.

www.mcspotlight.org
Shining the light on McYou Know Who and others.

www.moles.org
US organisation supporting communities resisting oil and
mining exploitation.

www.nader.org
Website of long-term US social critic, Ralph Nader.

www.transnationale.org
French site providing information about the practices of large
companies.

www.xs4all.nl/eo
The Corporate Europe Observatory research and campaign
group examines the economic and political power of
corporations.

HELPLINES

www.childline.co.uk
24/7 helpline for children in trouble or danger. (0800 1111)

www.getconnected.org.uk
Help and advice for young people.　　　　(0808 808 4994)

www.samaritans.org.uk
Suicide and depression support line.　　　(08457 909090)

HOMELESSNESS AND HOUSING

International

www.homeless-international.org
UK-based charity supporting community-led housing and
infrastructure-related development.

www.unchs.org
United Nations Centre for Human Settlements.

National
UNITED KINGDOM

www.bigissue.co.uk
www.crisis.org.uk
www.homeless.org.uk
www.homelesspages.org.uk
www.housing.org.uk
www.housingnet.co.uk
www.hungryandhomeless.co.uk
www.insidehousing.co.uk
www.london-connection.org.uk/welcome.html
www.ris.org.uk
www.shelter.org.uk
www.socialexclusionunit.gov.uk

UNITED STATES

www.habitat.org
www.nationalhomeless.org
www.realchangenews.org/issue/current/index.html

OTHER NATIONAL

www.bigissue.co.za	South Africa
www.cohre.org	Switzerland
www.eapn.org	Europe
www.feantsa.org	Europe

HUMAN RIGHTS

www.alphalink.net.au/~rez/Journey
Inspired by a 1997 federal report, Journey of Healing
attempts to address the issues raised by the Australian
Aboriginal Stolen Generations issue.

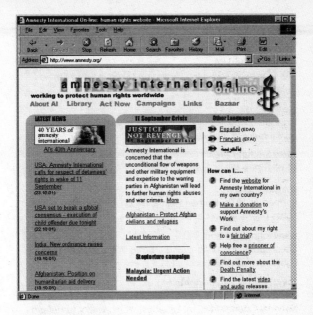

www.amnesty.org

With a million members and supporters in 162 countries and
territories, Amnesty International has been raising human
rights issues for over 40 years. **G**

www.amnesty.org.au	Australia
www.amnesty.ca	Canada
www.amnesty.ie	Ireland
www.amnesty.org.nz	New Zealand
www.amnesty.org.uk	United Kingdom
www.amnesty-usa.org	United States

www.burmacampaign.org.uk
Information about human rights abuse and the campaign for democracy in Burma.

www.ercomer.org
The European Research Centre on Migration and Ethnic Relations.

www.fdp.dk
Fight the Death Penalty, a Danish site that debates capital punishment in the US.

www.hrichina.org
Human Rights in China.

www.hrw.org
Formed in 1976, Human Rights Watch is the largest human rights organisation based in the US.

www.johnpilger.com
Site appraising the films and articles of the veteran human rights journalist.❻

www.liberty-human-rights.org.uk
Liberty, the human rights organisation, formerly known as the National Council for Civil Liberties, which works to defend and extend rights and freedoms in England and Wales.

www.reconciliation.org.au
The body formed to provide a continuing national focus for Australian reconciliation.

www.refugeecouncil.org.uk
With a mission to offer practical advice and promote refugees' rights, the Refugee Council is the largest UK organisation working with asylum seekers and refugees.

www.umn.edu/humanrts
Human rights library.

www.unifem.undp.org/index.htm
The United Nations Development Fund for Women works for women's empowerment and gender equality.

www.witness.org
Turning the Big Brother concept on its head by advocating the use of surveillance equipment to observe the observers, Witness believes that technological innovations such as the Internet and camcorders can be tools of positive social change. **❻**

LAW ENFORCEMENT

policeinternational.com
Links to law enforcement information from around the world.

www.police.uk
Links to UK online police forces.

www.prisonstudies.org
The International Centre for Prison Studies, from King's College, London.

PEACE AND DISARMAMENT
General sites
www.abolition2000.org
A Global Network to Eliminate Nuclear Weapons.

www.cnduk.org
The Campaign for Nuclear Disarmament works to rid the world of nuclear weapons and other weapons of mass destruction.

www.nucleardisarmament.org
The Nuclear Disarmament Party of Australia.

www.peace.net.nz
New Zealand's Peace Foundation.

www.peacewire.org
Providing information on peace and disarmament issues in
Canada.

www.warpeace.org
This site may not look particularly sophisticated, but here you
can listen to the latest edition and archives of Earthspan, a
weekly 30-minute radio report, plus excellent links.**ⓕ**

www.warresisters.org
Founded in 1923, the War Resisters League advocates non-
violence as the means by which a democratic society free of
war, racism, sexism, and human exploitation can be created.

www.world-nuclear.org
The World Nuclear Association represents the global nuclear
energy industry.

Landmines

www.canadianlandmine.com
The Canadian Landmine Foundation.

www.icbl.org
The International Campaign to Ban Landmines, including
Landmine Monitor report.

www.landmines.org / www.landmines.org.uk
UK and US Adopt-A-Minefield addressing the global
landmine crisis.**ⓕ**

www.protel.co.nz/calm
New Zealand Campaign Against Landmines.

www.sigov.si/itffund
International Trust Fund for Demining and Mine Victims
Assistance.

POPULATION

www.popexpo.net
Online exhibition explaining the issues of population stability from the Museum of Mankind in Paris.

www.popnet.org
The Population Reference Bureau provides directory links to population-related information.

www.prb.org
The Population Reference Bureau's main news and reference site.

RACISM

www.carf.demon.co.uk
Webpages of CARF magazine representing the Campaign Against Racism and Fascism.

www.cre.gov.uk
The UK Commission for Racial Equality.

www.ecri.coe.int
European Commission against Racism and Intolerance.

SOCIAL CHANGE

General sites

www.canadians.org
Website of the citizen's watchdog, The Council of Canadians.

www.changemakers.net
Site for social entrepreneurs who pioneer original solutions to social problems.

www.citizen.org
Raising public consciousness about social, trade, consumer and political issues in the US for over thirty years. **Ⓕ**

www.citizensconnection.net
Resources, links and publications relevant to social change from across the UK.

www.civicus.org
An international alliance dedicated to strengthening citizen action and civil society throughout the world.

www.foresight.gov.uk
UK government-led programme that aspires to bring different elements of society together to prepare for a better future.

www.slowfood.com
Slow Food makes Slow Cities.

www.socialplatform.org
The Platform of European Social NGOs brings together over 1700 direct member organisations, associations and other voluntary bodies at local, regional, national and European level, representing the interests of a wide range of civil society.

www.workingforchange.com
US site with suggestions about using working and shopping for the better.

www.worldrevolution.org
Seattle-based activist social movement for progressive social change.

Links: Shopping/Fair Trade and Ethical Consumerism

Think-tanks

See the thinking of the corporate and government influencing bodies that map out the way ahead for our societies.

www.adamsmith.org.uk
The Adam Smith Institute.

www.cbpp.org
Center on Budget and Policy Priorities, US.

www.demos.co.uk
Demos.

www.fabian-society.org.uk
The Fabian Society.

www.iea.org.uk
Institute of Economic Affairs.

www.ifs.org.uk
Institute for Fiscal Studies.

www.instituteofideas.com
Institute of Ideas.

www.ippr.org.uk
IPPR.

www.irc.essex.ac.uk
Institute for Social and Economic Research.

www.opendemocracy.net
Open Democracy.

www.policyalternatives.ca
The Canadian Centre for Policy Alternatives.

www.policybrief.org
Policy Brief.

www.psi.org.uk
Policy Studies Institute.

www.warwick.ac.uk/ier
Institute for Employment Research.

Links: Government and Politics/Politics

STRESS

www.isma.org.uk
The International Stress Management Association.

THIRD WORLD

www.twnside.org.sg
Third World Network.

www.undp.org
United Nations Development Programme.

VOLUNTEERING AND CHARITIES
Charities

bubl.ac.uk/uk/charities
Links to UK charities.

www.charitiesdirect.com
The Charities Direct database lists all UK charities and
provides Weblinks to each. Search alphabetically or by
name.

www.charityvillage.com
Source of information, news, jobs, services and resources for
the Canadian non-profit community.

Volunteering

Feel like it's time you put something back? There are many
and diverse ways of doing so. The Web is your best source
of volunteering information, both worldwide and locally.

www.btcv.org
British Trust for Conservation Volunteers.

www.navb.org.uk
UK National Association of Volunteer Bureaux, the
membership organisation for over 400 bureaux.

www.ncvo-vol.org.uk
The umbrella lobbying and research organisation for the
voluntary sector in England, with links to other UK
organisations.

www.volunteering.org.uk
The English National Centre for Volunteering provides
support for volunteer managers and organisations.

www.volwork.org.uk
Voluntary jobs for experienced managers and professionals
in the UK.

**There are many other volunteer sites on the Web. Here's a
selection:**

app.netaid.org/OV
www.aesop.org.au
www.beso.org
www.btcv.org
www.change.net
www.crossculturalsolutions.org
www.energizeinc.com
www.fido.com.au
www.hc-friends.org.uk
www.helping.org
www.govolunteer.com.au
www.iave.org
www.idealist.org
www.indepsec.org
www.iyv2001.org
www.pointsoflight.org
www.sja.org.uk/volunteer
www.unv.org
www.vds.org.uk
www.volunteer.ca
www.volunteer.org.au

www.volunteeringaustralia.org
www.volunteermatch.org
www.vso.org.uk
www.wrvs.org.uk

Links: Environmental Issues and World Concerns/Conflict/
        Disaster and Poverty Relief

WORKERS' RIGHTS

www.etuc.org
European Trade Union Confederation.

www.labourbehindthelabel.org
Support for international garment workers' rights.

www.theglobalalliance.org
Improving the workplace, lives and communities of workers
in global manufacturing and service companies.

www.tuc.org.uk
UK Trades Union Congress.

Film and the Movies

There are many thousands of film-related sites on the Web, representing all aspects of film watching, directing, producing and showing. To watch video clips, you'll need to have downloaded a media player, details of which can be found in the Music section.

GENERAL INFORMATION

film.guardian.co.uk
Film section of the popular UK newspaper site.

movies.mantraonline.com
Indian movie news.

oracleofbacon.org
The fun game whereby the Oracle links actors with other actors. **F**

www.afc.gov.au
The Australian Film Commission.

www.afionline.org
The American Film Institute.

www.bfi.org.uk
The British Film Institute, including *Sight and Sound* magazine. **F**

www.bigmoviezone.com
Information about IMAX films.

www.bollywoodpremiere.com
Information about India's Bollywood film industry.

www.chud.com
Thoughts and opinions at Cinematic Happenings Under Development.

www.cinemazine.com
Film theory and criticism.

www.cinescene.com
Non-commercial film commentary and criticism away from the mainstream.**❻**

www.filmcouncil.org.uk
UK Film Council.

www.filmfour.com
Interviews, reviews, shorts and exclusives.

www.filmosophy.org
A study of Film as Thinking.

www.filmreview.co.uk
Independent UK review site.

www.filmsite.org
In-depth commentary on the greatest films.**❻**

www.filmthreat.com
Championing independent and underground films.**❻**

www.futuremovies.co.uk
UK site dedicated to forthcoming releases.

www.movie-mistakes.com
Movie continuity errors, mistakes and general goofs.

www.mrqe.com
The Movie Review Query Engine pulls up reviews of most movies.

www.nitpickers.com
More movie errors.

www.nmpft.org.uk
UK National Museum of Photography, Film and Television, Bradford.

www.rivalquest.com/quotes
Quotes from your favourite films.

www.supercalafragalistic.com
Fun film review site.

www.tdfilm.com
Nearly 30,000 film links.

Other film information sites
movieweb.com
www.film.com
www.filmzone.com
www.script-o-rama.com

LISTINGS

search.yell.com/search/FilmSearch
UK film and cinema listings.

www.londonnet.co.uk/ln/out/ent/cinema.html
London Cinema and Movie Guide.

www.moviefone.com
US listing guide and ticket service.

www.tribute.ca
Movie showtimes and listings for Canada.

MAGAZINES

www.bollywoodonline.com
Latest news on Bombay's film scene.

www.boxoff.com
California-based magazine that has been reviewing classics,
flops and masterpieces for over 75 years.

www.brightlightsfilm.com
Movie analysis, history and commentary from *Bright Lights Film Journal*. **⑤**

www.empireonline.co.uk
Online edition of the popular UK magazine.

www.filmjournal.com
New York-based magazine.

www.gmagazine.com
Online version of India's best-selling film magazine.

www.hotdogmagazine.com
UK movie mag.

www.premiere.com
Exciting online presence of New York movie mag.

www.preview-online.com
UK-based international independent film and movie review magazine.

ARCHIVES, DIRECTORIES AND DATABASES

arts.anu.edu.au/Philosophy/videodata
Interesting Film and Philosophy Database.

www.allmovie.com
The All Movie Guide.

www.cinema.ucla.edu
UCLA's Film and Television Archive.

www.ifilm.com
Comprehensive movie database and video-on-demand library.

www.imdb.co.uk
Internet Movie Database covering over 200,000 titles.

FESTIVALS

www.filmfestivals.com
Directory of worldwide film festivals.

www.insidefilm.com
International film festival listings.

Links: Music/Media Players

Food and Drink

Along with love, sex and death, food and drink are probably the subjects closest to the fundamentals of life in which most people have an interest. Sustenance and libation are part of all our lives, and, yes, as you guessed, this intense interest is reflected on the Web.

Historically, food-related content is an acknowledged driver of new technologies: cookery programmes were among the first television shows to be broadcast in the 1930s, and, in computer terms, the distribution of recipes was one of the early demonstrations of how information could be shared over networks. Therefore it is not surprising to find a plethora of Websites providing a wide range of international recipes.

As well as within dedicated recipe sites, recipes are found dotted around most of the different types of food sites, from centralised food and drink portals, to celebrity chef personality sites, to sites catering specifically for organic foods or vegetarians.

Supermarkets were early exponents of e-commerce, and many were quick to establish themselves on the Web, with mixed results. There is currently an ongoing consolidation process, with some supermarkets closing down their Web-ordering services, while others seem to go from strength to strength. The difference between success and failure seems to depend on a number of factors, including the size of the catchment area, in terms of both population and geography, and how effectively e-commerce slots in with the rest of the business. The strategies applied by food stores vary, with some stores simply taking items off the shop shelves for home deliveries, and others establishing large-scale centralised warehouses. Either way, storage and distribution – involving the ability to stock products, and then to select, pack, and distribute them speedily and cost effectively – are key elements to success.

In essence, online supermarket shopping represents a speeding up, streamlining and formalising of an order and delivery process that many local supermarkets and corner shops have been offering for years, with the added convenience to the consumer of online 24/7 ordering and payment facilities.

Having said that, we believe that if your local supermarket is online, you probably already know about it, so no supermarket websites are listed here. However, many of the specialist food sites below have adopted the online shopping cart for their own services.

PORTALS

Many food and drink portals are unashamedly commercial, with tie-ins to food industry companies.

www.bbc.co.uk/food
Newsletters, recipes, tips and televisual tie-ins to celebrity chefs Rick Stein and Ainsley Harriott, and the Food and Drink programme.

www.epicurious.com
Food and Drink Internet vehicle of US publishers Condé Nast.

www.foodlines.com
Launched in 1996, this Canadian site provides general food information, including a section on healthy eating.

www.foodndrink.co.uk
This colourful magazine-style site provides comprehensive information across the range of food and drink topics for the UK and Ireland. Includes a useful directory of cookery schools and catering companies as well as a section dedicated to improving barbecue skills. Resident chef Emma invites you into her kitchen.**ⓕ**

www.sallys-place.com
Interesting information and articles about ethnic cuisine in this lively site that has been around since 1994, plus a dining directory covering the world's major cities.

www.taste.co.uk
This is a joint venture between Sainsbury's supermarket and Carlton media group, so it's no surprise to see the Taste CFN cable station schedules included, along with Sainsbury's online ordering facilities. However, this portal also includes a good UK restaurant guide, although the pop-up ads are an annoying distraction.

Other food and drink general portal sites
www.aboutfood.co.uk
www.cookingindex.com
www.foodtv.com
www.kitchenlink.com
www.tasteonline.co.uk

Alternative food sites
www.andreas.com/food.html
Ray's List of Weird and Disgusting Foods – Food for Thought.

www.tatfad.com
Guaranteed to make gourmets' and food connoisseurs' stomachs turn, The Alternative To Food And Drink takes a different approach with processed food and 'cheap nosh'. Reviews of convenience foods and supermarket booze.🅕

FOOD
Recipes
Like Horoscopes and News, you'll find recipes dotted all around the Web. They are particularly prevalent in general magazine and portal sites and in commercially-oriented sites aimed at women. Here's what may be the best recipe sites on the Web:

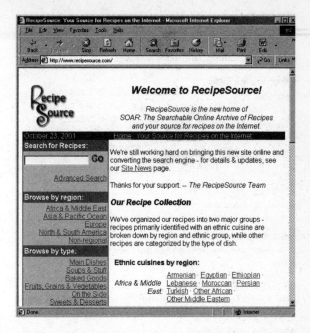

www.my-meals.com
A delightfully advertising-lite site that offers over 10,000 recipe ideas and creatively helps you to plan meals using the 'My Planning Centre' facility. You can also generate your own recipe and shopping lists.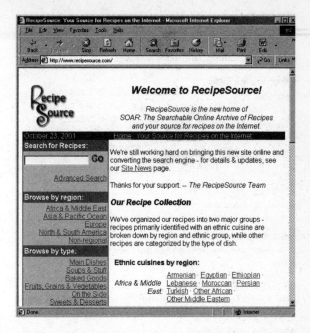

www.recipesource.com
Originally known as SOAR (The Searchable Online Archive of Recipes), Recipesource has grown since 1995 to a straightforward but impressive searchable database of over 70,000 recipes from around the world.

www.recipezaar.com
Colourful busy site with recipes subcategorized by cooking time and special diet requirements, as well as by the standard ingredients and cuisine types.

Other recipe sites

allrecipes.com
www.betterbaking.com
www.geocities.com/congocookbook
www.mealsforyou.com
www.recipecenter.com
www.the-astrology-cookbook.com

Celebrity and TV chefs

www.chefeasy.com
The Internet's first weekly video-on-demand cookery show.

www.deliaonline.com
Well-designed site from one of the UK's premier television chefs.

www.jamieoliver.net
Disappointing site that achieves little except to fuel the cult of personality surrounding this UK TV chef.

www.pbs.org/juliachild
America's original celebrity chef hosts this video-laden companion site to four PBS cookery series.

Restaurant guides

As well as sites dedicated to restaurant searches, such as those shown below, lists of local restaurants can also be found in travel guides.

WORLDWIDE

www.fodors.com/ri.cgi

www.foodtourist.com
www.restaurants.com

NATIONAL

Australia

www.bestrestaurants.com.au
www.eat-out.com.au
www.restaurant.org.au
www.restaurants.au.com

Canada

www.restaurant.ca

South Africa

www.styleguide.co.za

United Kingdom

www.cuisinenet.co.uk
www.local-restaurant.com
www.menumagazine.co.uk
www.menumaster.co.uk
www.pubsmaster.co.uk
www.restaurantreview.co.uk
www.restaurants.co.uk
www.theaa.com/getaway/restaurants/restaurant_home.jsp
www.ukrestaurantguide.com
www.where-to-eat.co.uk

United States

www.dinesite.com
www.latinrestaurants.com
www.restaurant-pages.com

Links: Travel/Travel Guidebooks

Organic food

www.greenmount.ac.uk/organic/olinks.htm
Link pages to other organic sites arranged under topic headings.

www.organicfood.co.uk
Organic lifestyle magazine from the UK. This site hosts the official Organic Food Federation Website and organic food chat zones. **ⓕ**

www.organicsnewzealand.org.nz
News and directories from the Organic Products Exporters of New Zealand.

www.soilassociation.org
The UK's Soil Association campaigns for organic food and farming and sustainable forestry. An online version of the Organic Directory is available here. This site also contains information about organic food and provides a comprehensive online library, including briefing and conference papers. **ⓕ**

Vegetarian and vegan

vegweb.com
Vegetarian resource guide, including recipes, hosted by About.com.

www.happycow.net
This fun site hosts the Happy Cow's idiosyncratic but informative Global Guide to vegetarian restaurants and health food stores.

www.ivu.org
The International Vegetarian Union has been promoting vegetarianism around the world since 1908. As well as being a global partnership directory, this site charts the history of the movement. **ⓕ**

www.vegansociety.com
UK Vegan Society news, information and link site.

www.vegdining.com
Useful worldwide vegetarian restaurant guide with reviews.

www.vegeats.com
Old-style Webpage of recipes and restaurant links. Includes links to vegetarian mailing lists and chat rooms.

www.vegetarian.com.au
Australian Vegetarian portal.

www.vegsoc.org
This well-designed site from the UK Vegetarian Society provides news, recipes, and a leisure and lifestyle directory which lists accommodation catering to vegetarians. **ⓕ**

Links: Shopping/Fair trade and ethical consumerism

National cuisines

Here are samples of some of the sites that concentrate solely on foods from one particular people or country:

www.chinatown-online.co.uk/pages/food/index.html
About Chinese food from Chinatown Online, the site that provides information about China and the Chinese community in the UK.

www.chopstix.co.uk
Well known popular Chinese food site.

www.eatjamaican.com
Information site about Jamaican food with worldwide list of bars and restaurants.

www.slowfood.com
Italy's slow food movement seems to be catching on globally. Links to the SloWeb round-the-clock food news and reviews site. **ⓕ**

www.thai-food.com/index.html
Restaurants worldwide and recipes for Thai food.

Specialist foods

www.aeb.org/eggcyclopedia/main_frame_page.html
Egg facts from the eggcyclopedia of the American Egg Board.

www.britishcheese.com
Another pun from the British Cheese Board. This site markets to the world via recipes and descriptions of different cheeses.

www.cheese.com
652-cheese database searchable by name, country and textures. The national cheese emporium of its day for those feeling esurient, or just simply peckish. And yes, they do have Limburger.

www.curryhouse.co.uk
Highly readable Web magazine for curry fans.

www.zenobianut.com
Nutty facts from this commercial importer of all kinds of nuts.

Healthy eating

www.3fatchicks.com
Low-fat cooking advice and dietary commentary from 3 Fat Chicks on a Diet.

www.cyberdiet.com
Counselling on diet, nutrition, exercise and fitness, plus access to dozens of discussion groups at this US site.

www.foodwatch.com.au
Very good, accessible information about healthy eating on this ad-free site from Australia, including an A to Z of Nutrition and an insight into the true meanings behind the food labels. **F**

www.mynutrition.co.uk
Personal online nutrition consultations are available from this interesting site, which also contains much useful free information.

www.nutrition.org
Site of the American Society for Nutritional Sciences,
publishers of the *Journal of Nutrition*.

www.nutrition.org.uk
The British Nutrition Foundation is a charitable organisation
which works in partnership with academic and research
institutes, the food industry, educators and government.

Food safety and hygiene

www.fightbac.org
Partnership for Food Safety Education, a US public-private
coalition dedicated to educating the public about safe food
handling to help reduce foodborne illness.

www.foodlink.org.uk
The result of a coalition between various UK government
departments, health institutes and local authorities, Foodlink
organises Food Safety Week, which aims to help people
understand the causes of food poisoning and to provide
advice about the basic precautions which can be taken to
avoid it.

www.foodsafety.gov
US government food safety advice and information hub.

DRINK
Beverages

Many of the tea and coffee sites are sponsored by suppliers,
but they contain some good, entertainingly delivered
information.

COFFEE

www.coffee.com
Interesting site tracing the story of coffee beans from source
to cup.

www.coffeekid.com
'A Coffee Lover's Obsession Site' including meditations on espresso and VacPot brewing.

www.coffeereview.com
The coffee equivalent to wine-tasting at this coffee sampling site.

www.coffeescience.org
Coffee Science Source from the US National Coffee Association provides up-to-date information on coffee, caffeine and health.

www.ineedcoffee.com/us/mission
Coffee-related information, instruction and entertainment.🅕

www.realcoffee.co.uk
Information and ordering for tea and coffee.

www.smellthecoffee.com
Wake up and ... at this consumer and trade site, with a somewhat limited worldwide directory of coffee shops, cafés and cybercafés.

www.virtualcoffee.com
Online magazine for the coffee consumer.

TEA

www.liptont.com
Information and promotion from Lipton.

www.stashtea.com
Informative but old-fashioned site from a US-based commercial specialist tea company.

www.tea.co.uk
Umbrella site from the British Tea Council, with links to its other information sites.🅕

www.teahealth.co.uk
Site stressing the health implications of tea from the British Tea Council.

www.tealand.com
Organic, traditional, herbal and medicinal tea information and ordering at this US site.

www.tetley.com
Information sites for Canada, UK and US from Tetley, the tea-folk.

www.time-for-tea.com
Another info-promo site from Lipton.

www.twinings.com
A formal history of tea from the well known tea brand, with a link to their UK Website.

www.whittard.com
Tea and Coffee information and purchasing.

Alcoholic drinks
BEER

realbeer.co.nz
News, information archives, and articles about Australian and New Zealand beers.

www.beerbarons.co.uk
Beer information, brewery directory and online ordering of world beers for home delivery.

www.brewing.co.nz
New Zealand Brewers Network.

www.camra.org.uk
Campaign For Real Ale, an independent voluntary consumer organisation which saved real ale from extinction in the UK, with branches throughout the UK and world-wide.

COCKTAILS

hotwired.lycos.com/cocktail
Recipes, history and commentary for a wide selection of cocktails.

www.drinkboy.com
Extensive cocktail recipes, together with articles and reference library.

WHISKY

www.smws.com
The Scottish Whisky Association

www.whiskyportal.com
Links to whisky producers worldwide.

WINE

www.cyberbacchus.com
Directory-style US wine portal.

www.wawine.com.au
Group site for Western Australian wineries, also including general information on the Australian wine industry.

www.wine.co.za
Background information to the South African wine industry, including climate, cultivars, regions, soils and viticulture.**F**

www.winedine.co.uk
Wine, restaurants and travel e-zine, now in its seventh year, with over 1,000 archived articles.

www.winefocus.com
Useful wine resource and information link site, with good selection of tours and travel, cellars and racking, and events links.

www.winelink.com.au
Wines, wineries and wine regions of Australia.

www.wine-lovers-page.com
Huge resource for anyone who cares about wine, including sections on wine and politics, wine label decoder, articles by numerous wine writers, a wine lexicon, discussion groups and chat rooms. **ⓕ**

www.winespectator.com
News and articles about the world of wine at this US site.

Other wine sites
decanter.com
www.wine.com
www.wineanswers.com
www.wine-pages.com
www.wines.com

Wine routes and tours
www.wineroute.co.za
Details of the Stellenbosch Wine Route, the first wine route in South Africa, covering forty-four cellars.

www.yarravalleywinerytours.com.au
Company offering commercial wine tours in Australia.

Buying wine
www.greatgrog.co.uk
www.winealley.com
www.winereleasedate.com
www.winesearcher.com
www.wineshop.it

Gardens and Gardening

PORTALS

Gardening portals generally cater primarily to their national audiences and to those of other regions sharing the same climatic conditions. Regardless of their target audience, the portals usually follow the same model in terms of content, although the format and design qualities will vary, influenced by such considerations as the size of potential readership, the range of products and services on offer, and the level of commercial sponsorship involved.

These sites usually seek to strike a balance between the entertaining provision of information, and a commercial drive that is essentially selling products and services. Generally, the more commercial the site, the greater the level of design and navigational slickness, which can sometimes lend the sites a kind of empty blandness.

Gardening portals are often created in the style of an on-line magazine, as are their equivalents in the subject areas of food and drink, some 'women's sites', and, to a lesser extent, certain health portals. As with portals for the other subjects, some gardening portals are independent, while others are part of a greater linked network of Websites, with a common format and design style across the network. Some may also be a tie-in with an established print magazine.

Gardening portals frequently include a link to an online shop offering gardening equipment, accessories and, sometimes, plants and seeds. An alternative to a Website shop may be a products and services resources directory, linking to associated suppliers. Book reviews and purchasing options may also be included. Sites of this nature are a kind of combined magazine and catalogue.

Gardening portals also provide 'ask-the-expert' advice sections, with specific questions posed by visitors to the sites. This is one aspect where Web portals have the potential to go beyond their print counterparts, building on and extending the principles of information sharing, with the creation of interactive gardening communities. These are hosted by a particular portal, with tips and suggestions being exchanged by members within the electronic community in the form of bulletin boards, chat or discussion forums, rather than one expert, or a panel of experts, providing the replies. Extending this principle, some portals may be affiliated to, or have links with, local or online gardening clubs. Some portals may also seek to establish a direct link to regular site visitors by offering e-mail newsletters.

Additional facilities offered by gardening portals include plant and product reviews and news, guides and tips, seasonal planting and garden maintenance suggestions, notification of regional and national events, and garden design services and advice. The more serious portals may provide a plant index, photo galleries, and possibly a library or articles archive.

Here's a selection of the gardening portals we particularly liked:

Australia

www.gardensonline.com.au
www.global-garden.com.au
www.lebepsgarden.zipworld.com.au

Canada

www.canadiangardening.com
www.gardenforever.com
www.icangarden.com

Ireland

www.garden.ie

New Zealand

gardens.co.nz
www.bestgardening.com

South Africa
www.gardensofafrica.com

United Kingdom
www.armchair-gardening.co.uk
www.bbc.co.uk/gardening
www.expertgardener.com
www.fantasy-gardening.com
www.gardenweb.com
www.gonegardening.co.uk
www.internetgarden.co.uk
www.wildflowergardening.co.uk
www.wildlifeforever.net

United States
gardening.com
greenprints.com
www.backyardgardener.com
www.floriculture.com
www.garden.org❻
www.gardenguides.com
www.gardenmag.com
www.hortmag.com
www.ngb.org
www.windowbox.com

ORGANIC GARDENING

Many of the mainstream portals provide sections about organic gardening. However, there are a growing number of sites
dedicated to promoting environmentally friendly, organic
methods.

Australia
www.backyardorganicgardening.com

www.organicdownunder.com
www.thevegetablepatch.com

United Kingdom

www.earth-to-earth.com
www.hdra.org.uk
www.organic.cwc.net

United States

www.organicgardening.com

CLUBS AND SOCIETIES

Gardening clubs, associations and societies exist in vast numbers and offer varying degrees of services and activities for their members. Here's a small selection of those that have a broad appeal.

www.botanicalsociety.org.za
www.bulbsociety.com
www.gardenclubs.org.au
www.rhs.org.uk

PERSONAL SITES

Many gardeners post online details of the seasonal developments in their own gardens. These kinds of sites can sometimes make a refreshing change from the more commercially oriented general garden portals.

colleenscorner.com/Garden.html**F**
www.benchmark-garden.co.uk
www.gardendigest.com
www.mooseyscountrygarden.com
www.shoalhaven.net.au/~romaine

SHOPPING

As well as the shopping sections within the general gardening portals, there are a huge number of sites providing commercial resources for gardeners, ranging from accessories and garden implements, to fertilisers and feed, and garden ornaments. Many also provide online purchasing of plants and seeds. However, there can be importation restrictions on these, so it is advisable to purchase in your own region, or to check fully before purchasing.

Australia

yates.com.au
www.gardeningnow.com.au

New Zealand

www.infogarden.co.nz

United Kingdom

www.blooms-online.com
www.crocus.co.uk
www.dreamgardens.co.uk
www.e-garden.co.uk
www.gardenersworld.beeb.com
www.gardenworld.co.uk
www.gonegardening.com
www.greenfingers.com
www.nickys-nursery.co.uk
www.wildflowers.co.uk

United States

www.burpee.com
www.gardennet.com

BOTANICAL GARDENS AND ARBORETA

Many botanical gardens and arboreta now have Websites.

These vary from being well designed and accessible to the general public, to those which are catering primarily for the academic botany community and which tend to be text-dominated. We have selected sites from some of the best known botanical organisations, and for gardens open to the public.

Worldwide

www.botany.net/IDB/subject/botgard.html
The Internet Directory for Botany, a huge links site, has excellent worldwide links for most Arboreta and Botanical Gardens.

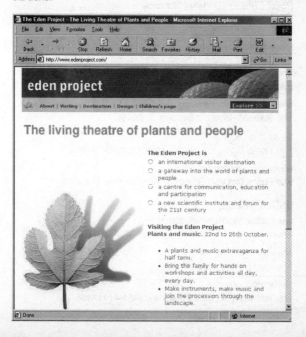

National
AUSTRALIA
www.anbg.gov.au
Australian National Botanic Gardens, Canberra.

CANADA
www.botanique.com
Lists more than 2,300 gardens, arboreta and nature sites in North America.

www.rbg.ca
Royal Botanic Gardens, Ontario.

UNITED KINGDOM
www.edenproject.com
This Cornwall-based millennium project promotes the understanding and responsible management of the vital relationship between plants, people and resources. ⑤

www.gardenofwales.org.uk
The National Botanic Garden of Wales.

www.rbge.org.uk
The Royal Botanic Garden, Edinburgh, Scotland.

www.rbgkew.org.uk
The Royal Botanic Gardens, Kew, Surrey, England.

UNITED STATES
www.atlantabotanicalgarden.org
Atlanta Botanical Garden, Georgia.

www.mobot.org
Missouri Botanical Gardens.

www.ntbg.org
The National Tropical Botanical Garden, Hawaii.

www.nybg.org
New York Botanical Garden.

Links: Nature/Aquaria and Zoos

VISITING OTHER GARDENS

www.barnsdalegardens.co.uk
Barnsdale, Rutland, Leicestershire, creation of Geoff
Hamilton, Britain's best-loved television gardener.

www.gardenvisit.com
Details of gardens to visit worldwide.

www.museumgardenhistory.org
The UK's Museum of Garden History, London.

www.nationaltrust.org.uk
The UK's National Trust preserves buildings and gardens.

www.ngs.org.uk
UK National Gardens Scheme.

PLANTS AND PLANT TYPES

General directories and indexes

plants.usda.gov/plants
www.botany.com
www.floridata.com

Specific plant types

BONSAI

www.bonsai-bci.com
www.bonsaiprimer.com
www.bonsaiweb.com

CACTUS

www.cactus-mall.com

HERBS

www.herbnet.com
www.herbsociety.co.uk

ROSE

www.everyrose.com
www.rosarian.com
www.rose.org
www.roses.co.uk
www.timelessroses.com

Genealogy

One of the most popular application areas on the Internet, genealogical research lends itself perfectly to the archival properties of the Web. While currently used primarily by those investigating their family histories throughout the English speaking countries of the UK, North America, and Australia and New Zealand, genealogical Black and Jewish resources are growing in popularity and purpose, as are those for people of European descent.

The desire to find out where we come from and who our ancestors were has always been there, and the Internet is a real boon, as the speed of searching for genealogical information over the Internet makes it easier to track down and detect relevant data worldwide. It also plays a vital role in improving communications between connected families, with e-mail helping the contacting and sharing aspects of research.

The sites below include resources such as war grave records, cemetery records, public records offices and national archives that can prove invaluable in tracing genealogical connections. Many of the sites that concentrate on genealogy as a subject provide regular free e-mail newsletters to keep researchers up-to-date with the latest developments.

GENEALOGY SITES

ccharity.com
Christine's Black American Genealogy Website.

genealogypro.com
For those who need professional help, this worldwide database of genealogical services may point you in the right direction.

olivetreegenealogy.com
North American resource including passenger lists and military data, with Huguenot and Mohawk sections.

www.afrigeneas.com
Well designed site for African-Americans.

www.convictcentral.com
This site offers an interesting and amusing route to locating
that convict ancestor so desired by many Australian families,
and makes a convincing case for its claim to be 'the
definitive site for convict research'.

www.cyndislist.com
Highly popular and comprehensive genealogy site with over
90,000 categorised and indexed links.❻

www.downtown.co.nz/genealogy
New Zealand Genealogy Search Engine.

www.earl.org.uk/familia
Familia, a useful guide to genealogical resources in public
libraries for the UK and Ireland, was created by EARL: the
Consortium for Public Library Networking.

www.familyrecords.gov.uk
Official government data from the UK Public Records
Office.

www.familysearch.org
US site detailing Mormon records.

www.familytreemaker.com
Product of Genealogy.com.

www.firstfamilies2001.net.au
Database and collection of stories about Australians past
and present that aspires to be the Australian equivalent of
the English *Domesday Book* of 1082.❻

www.genealogy.com
Part of US A&E Television Networks, along with
HistoryChannel.com and Biography.com.

www.genealogy-geneology.com
So good they named it twice? Site sponsored by namesake Genealogy.com.

www.genealogy.ie
Site of Celtic origins, a pay-for service helping people trace their Irish roots.

www.genealogy.org
Long-standing genealogy portal. Part of Rootsweb.com.

www.genealogy.org.nz
The New Zealand Society of genealogists offers advice about how to embark upon genealogical research.

www.genealogylinks.net
Invaluable link site to over 9,000 international resources.

www.genealogypages.com
Directory style link to some helpful sites.

www.genopro.com
A free downloadable program that allows family genealogical and medical histories to be visualised. Photos can be incorporated and the results can be posted on the Net.

www.genuki.org.uk
Links to UK and Ireland resources.

www.indiaman.com
Website of the hard-copy magazine for people researching their ancestry who are of British and European origin in India and Southern Asia.

www.jewishgen.org
JewishGen's online *Family Tree of the Jewish People* contains data on nearly two million individuals. This site also hosts the International Association of Jewish Genealogical Societies, which provides links throughout the world.

www.origins.net
Host to English Origins and Scottish Origins.

www.polishroots.com
As the name suggests, this site is for those researching their Polish ancestry.

www.sog.org.uk
The Society of Genealogists is a London-based charity whose objectives are to 'promote, encourage and foster the study, science and knowledge of genealogy'. Includes library and lecture series details.

www.ukgenealogy.co.uk
Many, but certainly not all, British surnames by county.

www.usgenweb.org
US genealogical information by state and county.

www.worldgenweb.org
Extensive worldwide links to data via this impressive portal of the WorldGenWeb Project. Includes country-by-country online data repositories for queries, family histories, and source records as well as being a resource centre to identify other online databases and resources to assist researchers. **F**

Other genealogy sites

genealogytoday.com
members.aol.com/rprost/passenger.htm
web.liswa.wa.gov.au/geneocent.html
www.accessgenealogy.com
www.mytrees.com
www.prov.vic.gov.au
www.surnameweb.org

OTHER USEFUL SITES

www.cwgc.org
The Commonwealth War Graves Commission's Website.

www.findagrave.com
Snappily named site that includes a 'Find Famous Graves'
option to help you track down the remains of celebrities,
authors, artists and similar. Also provides searches against
2.5 million graves of the not-so-famous. ❻

www.ingeneas.com
Passenger and immigration records for Canada.

www.interment.net
Cemetery Records Online accesses around 3 million records
from approaching 5,000 cemeteries in the English-speaking
world.

www.islandregister.com
Records for Prince Edward Island, Canada.

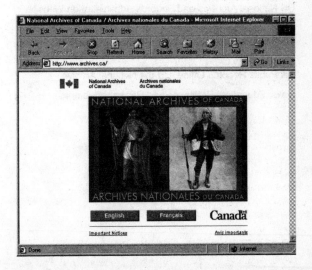

NATIONAL ARCHIVES

proni.nics.gov.uk
Public Records Office of Northern Ireland.

www.archives.ca
This elegantly designed site of the National Archives of
Canada includes genealogical records. **ⓕ**

www.archives.govt.nz/index.html
New Zealand's national archives, but without specific
genealogical resources.

www.naa.gov.au
The National Archives of Australia.

www.nara.gov
US National Archives and Records Administration Website.

www.national.archives.gov.za
The National Archives of South Africa.

www.pro.gov.uk
UK Public Records Office and the National Archive.

Links: Education, Reference and Research/Libraries

Government and Politics

GOVERNMENT

Usually well constructed, well designed and accessible, official government and parliamentary sites generally provide an opening into a world of useful information about the policies and initiatives that influence our lives.

Parliaments

NATIONAL

pm.gc.ca	Canadian Prime Minister
www.aph.gov.au	Australia
www.parl.gc.ca	Canada
www.gov.ie/oireachtas	Ireland
www.poli.govt.nz	New Zealand
www.parliament.gov.za	South Africa
www.parliament.uk	United Kingdom
www.scottish.parliament.uk	Scotland
www.wales.gov.uk	Wales
www.prime-minister.gov.uk	United Kingdom Prime Minister
www.house.gov	United States House of Representatives
www.senate.gov	United States Senate
www.whitehouse.gov	United States President

INTERNATIONAL

www.comparlhq.org.uk
The Commonwealth Parliamentary Association works to promote knowledge and understanding of the constitutional, legislative, economic, social and cultural systems within a parliamentary democratic framework.

www.ipu.org
Inter-Parliamentary Union, the world organisation of sovereign states, established in 1889.

Europe

stars.coe.fr
Parliamentary Assembly of the Council of Europe (PACE).

www.europarl.eu.int
The European Parliament.

National governments

AUSTRALIA

www.fed.gov.au
Concentrated body of Australian Commonwealth
Government information with links to over 500 Websites.

www.go.vic.gov.au
Victoria Government online resource centre.

www.govonline.gov.au
National Office for the Information Economy, coordinating
government policy on electronic commerce, online services
and the Internet.

www.onlinewa.com.au
Western Australia information and services.

CANADA

canada.gc.ca
Entry point to the main Government of Canada public
Website. The A to Z Index provides links to hundreds of
subsites.

www.statcan.ca
Canada's Statistical Agency, profiling population, economy,
resources, society and culture.

IRELAND

www.irlgov.ie
The Government of Ireland.

NEW ZEALAND

www.e-government.govt.nz
The New Zealand online government and services programme.

www.govt.nz
This official gateway to New Zealand government provides access to government services information and employment opportunities, government agency details and an overview of New Zealand.

www.nzgovtdirectory.com
Comprehensive guide to New Zealand's political and public sectors.

SOUTH AFRICA

www.gov.za
The South African government online Website provides information about government departments, provinces and other government bodies from one central portal.

www.polity.org.za
South African government information, including press statements.

UNITED KINGDOM

www.dag-business.gov.uk
Direct Access Government for Business, providing easy access to regulatory guidance and forms published on government Websites.

www.inlandrevenue.gov.uk
News and information on tax and national insurance matters.

www.statistics.gov.uk
Official UK national statistics.

www.tagish.co.uk/tagish/links
Useful Directory of UK Government Offices' Websites,
including those for local and regional authorities.

www.ukonline.gov.uk
Government-driven initiative to get UK individuals and
businesses online.

UNITED STATES
congress.org
Find and contact elected officials regarding issues and
legislation.

www.census.gov
Data about the people and economy of the US.

www.fedworld.gov
Access to government databases and Websites from the US
Dept of Commerce.

www.firstgov.gov
Official site for US Government information, services,
transactions and forms.

www.hicitizen.com
Aims to make interactions with government easier, friendlier
and more convenient when, for example, paying taxes,
getting a passport or registering a vehicle.

www.state.gov
US Department of State.

EUROPE
europa.eu.int/comm
The European Commission.

ue.eu.int
Council of the European Union.

www.coe.int
Council of Europe.

Other European sites
amue.lf.net
The Association for the Monetary Union of Europe.

www.euro.ecb.int
Details of the Euro from the European Central Bank.**Ⓕ**

www.europointcom.co.uk/PREU
Political resources connected with the European Union.

DEFENCE, SECURITY AND STABILITY

www.assemblee-ueo.org
The Parliamentary Assembly of the Western European Union
monitors security and defence issues.

www.naa.be
NATO Parliamentary Assembly of the 19 NATO nations and
17 associate parliaments.

www.nato.int
Official Website of the North Atlantic Treaty Organisation,
securing the Euro-Atlantic region.**Ⓕ**

www.osce.org
Organization for Security and Co-operation in Europe.

www.un.org
The United Nations is tasked with maintaining international
peace and security, solving international economic, social,
cultural and humanitarian problems and promoting respect
for human rights and fundamental freedoms.

POLITICS

We've generally avoided the official Websites of the many national political parties in favour of interesting political commentary, observation or issue sites.

General

www.geocities.com/CapitolHill/Lobby/4192
Links to Leftist Parties of the World.

www.klipsan.com/elecnews.htm
Election Notes provides information about political voting worldwide.

www.politicalresources.net
Links to political sites worldwide.

NATIONAL

Canada

politicswatch.com
Commentary and information about Canadian politics, including a daily review of political and national news, voter resources and details of political parties and leaders.🄕

www.afn.ca
The Assembly of First Nations.

www.cpac.ca
Canada's political television channel provides live streaming video of its entire broadcast schedule.

United Kingdom

www.charter88.org.uk
Independent organisation working for democratic reform of the UK political system.

www.e-politix.com
UK political commentary portal.🄕

www.politicsdirect.com
Links to parliamentary publications, press releases and
information from public affairs consultancy.

www.yougov.com
Online opinion polls and political research.

United States
www.opensecrets.org
Spilling the beans about US political funding.**ⓕ**

www.politicsonline.com
Using the Web for politics.

Links: Environmental Issues and World Concerns/Social
Change/Think-tanks

Health and Medical

There are many helpful medical and health information sites available which can prove to be useful starting points when you wish to find out more about a health matter. For instance, arming yourself with some basic information prior to a visit to a GP can make the discussion more rewarding. Similarly, many patients feel reassured when they can look up the details of prescribed medicines on the Web, and there are authoritative online medical directories, dictionaries and encyclopaedias which can provide this sort of information.

In theory the Web has democratised access to information about health matters, empowering the public by providing information that formerly would have been available only to the medical profession. While there's some truth in the observation that Web-based health information brings the potentially positive result of a better informed medical consumer, it also provides the possibility that such information may be misinterpreted and cause alarm.

Contextualisation of symptoms is often all-important when making a medical diagnosis, and without the proper knowledge and understanding, it can be easy to reach the wrong conclusions. Beware the 'home doctor syndrome' when it seems that you have every symptom of that rare tropical disease, yet you've never even left your home town. It should go without saying that it is advisable to use Web-based information in conjunction with professional medical advice, rather than relying upon it as the sole means of diagnosis or treatment.

It's also worth remembering that any information on the Web could be incomplete, incorrect, misleading or unsubstantiated. The liberty that the Web delivers to freely post information also means that there is often little qualification or independent assessment of the advice provided, and, as yet, few legal controls, particularly in relation to alternative medicines, nutritional supplements, cosmetic surgery, weight loss and fitness information. There can be no guarantees as to accuracy, appropriateness or quality, particularly when commercial gain is involved. It's wise to check the credentials of each source and to consult only reputable suppliers or advisors. Bear in mind that, generally, there are no miracle cures.

Support groups for specific medical conditions can often provide an invaluable source of help, advice and information. However, it is important to exercise caution concerning anecdotal evidence and personal experiences. Sites from independent institutions and charities specialising in particular areas of disease or medicine are generally reliable.

PORTALS

General health portal sites can prove to be a useful entry point for broad health and fitness issues. They come in all shapes and sizes, ranging from the openly commercial to the informative, but sometimes cautiously non-committal government and national health service sites.

Australia

www.betterhealth.vic.gov.au
www.emedical.com.au
www.healthanswers.com.au
www.healthinsite.gov.au
www.healthnetwork.com.au

Canada

www.canadian-health-network.ca
www.hc-sc.gc.ca/english
www.healthfrontier.com
www.medbroadcast.com
www.sympatico.ca/Contents/Home+Family/health.html

New Zealand

www.everybody.co.nz

www.nzdoctor.co.nz
www.nzhis.govt.nz

South Africa

www.edoc.co.za
www.health.co.za
www.health-e.org.za
www.healthzone.co.za
www.medline.co.za

United Kingdom

www.bbc.co.uk/health
www.healthindex.co.uk
www.healthinfocus.co.uk
www.healthnet.org.uk
www.medisearch.co.uk
www.netdoctor.co.uk
www.nhs.uk
www.nhsdirect.nhs.uk
www.patient.co.uk
www.patientsupport.org.uk
www.surgerydoor.co.uk
www.tagish.co.uk/Links/#health
www.wellbeing.com

United States

www.ahd.com
www.altruisbiomedical.net
www.ask-the-doc.com
www.drkoop.com
www.healthcentral.com
www.healthfinder.gov
www.healthtalk.com
www.healthwide.com
www.intelihealth.com

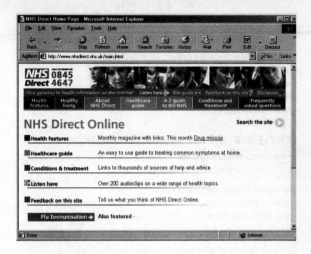

www.mayohealth.org
www.medavenue.com
www.medicalanswer.com

HEALTH NEWS

Getting the inside track on health news and developments can be a useful way of keeping informed about medical and health issues.

www.health-news.co.uk
www.ivanhoe.com
www.quackwatch.com
www.who.int

MEDICAL SEARCH AND REFERENCE

Useful for finding a local hospital, or for looking up that strangely named drug your doctor just prescribed.

www.achoo.com
www.childhospice.org.uk
www.graylab.ac.uk/omd
www.healthcyclopedia.com
www.healthy.net
www.hospitalweb.co.uk
www.medic8.com
www.nlm.nih.gov

COMPLEMENTARY AND ALTERNATIVE MEDICINE

www.acupuncture.org.uk
British Acupuncture Council.

www.alternativemedicine.com
Good drop-down menu facilities for locating analysis of
specific problems and conditions at this magazine site.

www.alt-med.co.uk
Links directory of alternative medicine.

www.aor.org.uk
UK Association of Reflexologists.

www.drlockie.com
Homeopathic advice and services.

www.hans.org
Health Action Network Society of Canada.

www.healingwithnutrition.com
Nutrition as the basis of a healthy life at this US site.

www.homeopathyhome.com
Useful links and directory site.

www.internethealthlibrary.com
Alternative medicine, complementary therapy and natural
health care resources from the UK.

www.int-fed-aromatherapy.co.uk
International Federation of Aromatherapists.

www.medical-acupuncture.co.uk
The British Medical Acupuncture Society provides
information for patients and professionals.

www.naturalhealth.co.za
South African Health Network.

www.the-cma.org.uk
Complementary Medical Association.

Osteopathy and massage

www.amtamassage.org
www.ancientmassage.com
www.golten.co.uk
www.maa.org.au
www.massageresource.com
www.massagetherapy.co.uk
www.osteopathy.org.uk
www.reikiassociation.org.uk
www.shiatsu.org

ONLINE DRUG DISPENSARY AND HEALTHCARE PRODUCTS

While good prices and the convenience of home delivery can
be found for general over-the-counter soothers and palliatives,
caution should be exercised when ordering prescription drugs
using these services.

www.allcures.com
www.anymed.com
www.drugdispensary.com
www.netchemist.co.nz
www.pharmacy2u.co.uk

SPECIFIC HEALTH ISSUES AND DISEASES

The sites below are possibly the most useful and rewarding aspect of health on the Web, providing good detailed information from health-related charities and institutions, and support and shared experiences from support networks and organisations for sufferers of specific medical conditions.

Alcoholism

www.aaindia.org
Alcoholics Anonymous India.

www.aa-uk.org.uk
Independently-run site with useful worldwide links.

www.alcohol.org.nz
Alcohol Advisory Council of New Zealand.

www.alcoholicsanonymous.org.au
Alcoholics Anonymous Australia.

www.alcoholics-anonymous.org
US-based site with international links.

www.alcoholics-anonymous.org.uk
Alcoholics Anonymous UK.

Alzheimer's Disease

www.alz.co.uk
Alzheimer's Disease International, umbrella organisation of 58 associations.

www.alz.org
US Alzheimer's Association.

www.alzheimer.ca
Alzheimer Society Canada.

www.alzheimer-europe.org
Alzheimer Europe, raising awareness of all forms of dementia.

www.alzheimers.org
US Alzheimer's Disease Education and Referral Center.

www.alzheimers.org.au
Alzheimer's Association of Australia.

www.alzheimers.org.uk
The UK Alzheimer's Society.

Arthritis

arthritisinsight.com
Informative and friendly US community site created by and for people with Arthritis.

www.arc.org.uk
UK Arthritis Research Campaign.

www.arthritis.ca
The Arthritis Society Canada.

www.arthritis.org
US Arthritis Foundation.

www.curearthritis.org
US Arthritis National Research Foundation.

www.preventarthritis.org
The Arthritis Research Institute of America.

www.span.com.au/arthritis/organisation.html
The Arthritis Foundation of Australia.

Asthma

www.aaaai.org
American Academy of Allergy, Asthma & Immunology Online.

www.aafa.org
Asthma and Allergy Foundation of America.

www.asthma.org.uk
UK National Asthma Campaign.

www.asthmaaustralia.org.au
Association of all the Asthma associations throughout Australia.

www.asthmanz.co.nz
The Asthma and Respiratory Foundation of New Zealand.

www.asthmasociety.com
Asthma Society of Canada.

www.cnac.net
Canadian Network for Asthma Care.

www.efanet.org
European Federation of Asthma and Allergy Association.

www.ginasthma.com
Global Initiative for Asthma.

www.iacouncil.com
International Asthma Council.

www.nationalasthma.org.au
National Asthma Council, Australia.

Cancer

cancernet.nci.nih.gov
CancerNet, a service of the US National Cancer Institute.

oncolink.upenn.edu
Information from the University of Pennsylvania Cancer Center.

www.actioncancer.org
Northern Ireland's cancer charity.

www.cancer.ca
Canadian Cancer Society.

www.cancer.org
American Cancer Society.

www.cancer.org.au
Australian Cancer Society.

www.cancerbacup.org.uk
Authoritative information from CancerBACUP, the UK's
leading cancer information service.

www.cancerfacts.com
US online resource for patients, their families and carers.

www.cancerindex.org
Information and links about the many different types of
cancer, including childhood cancers.

www.cancerlinksusa.com
Links to information about all types of cancer.

www.cancernz.org.nz
Cancer Society of New Zealand.

www.graylab.ac.uk/cancerweb.html
Large number of links to cancer-related sites.

www.icr.ac.uk
University of London's Institute of Cancer Research.

www.imperialcancer.co.uk
Imperial Cancer Research Fund.

www.macmillan.org.uk
UK information, treatment and care charity.

www.mariecurie.org.uk
Marie Curie UK Cancer Care charity.

www.uicc.ch
International Union Against Cancer.

BREAST CANCER

www.actionbreastcancer.org
Breast cancer charity based in Northern Ireland.

www.bci.org.au
Australia Breast Cancer Institute, New South Wales.

www.breast.cancer.ca
Canadian Breast Cancer Research Initiative.

www.breastcancer.net
Latest news on breast cancer research and treatment.

www.breastcancercare.org.uk
UK support and information charity.

www.breastcancerfund.org
US non-profit organisation formed to accelerate the response
to breast cancer.

www.nabco.org
US National Alliance of Breast Cancer Organizations.

www.nationalbreastcancer.org
US National Breast Cancer Foundation.

www.natlbcc.org
US National Breast Cancer Coalition.

www.nbcc.org.au
Source National Breast Cancer Centre, Australia.

PROSTATE CANCER

www.prostate.org.au
Prostate Cancer Foundation of Australia.

www.prostatecancer.on.ca
Prostate Cancer Research Foundation of Canada.

www.prostatehealth.org
A US information Service for patients and health care
professionals.

www.prostatehealth.org.au
Education site from the Australian Prostate Cancer
Collaboration, with funding from Lions International Club of
Australia.

www.prostatepointers.org
US prostate cancer information site.

TESTICULAR CANCER
**hcd2.bupa.co.uk/fact_sheets/Mosby_factsheets/testicular_
cancer.html**
Fact sheet from BUPA, the worldwide healthcare company.

www.acor.org/TCRC
The Testicular Cancer Resource Center.

www.orchid-cancer.org.uk
The Orchid Cancer Appeal is a UK charity funding research
into diagnosis, prevention and treatment of prostate and
testicular cancer.

www.tcrc-uk.co.uk
UK testicular cancer support group.

Diabetes
www.diabetes.co.za
Diabetes site from South Africa, supported by Roche.

www.diabetes.org
American Diabetes Association.

www.diabetes.org.au
Information from the Diabetes Centre, Queen Elizabeth
Hospital, South Australia.

www.diabetes.org.uk
Formerly the British Diabetic Association, Diabetes UK is a diabetes research and campaign charity.

www.diabetic.org.uk
Diabetes Insight, an independent information site from the UK.

www.drinet.org
Diabetes Research Institute, based in US.

www.insulin-pumpers.org.uk
Part of an international charity promoting the use of insulin pump therapy to treat diabetes.

www.sada.org.za
South African Diabetes Association.

Heart and stroke

www.americanheart.org
American Heart Association.

www.bhf.org.uk
British Heart Foundation.

www.heartandstroke.ca
Heart and Stroke Foundation, Canada.

www.heartfoundation.co.za
Heart Foundation, South Africa.

www.heartfoundation.com.au
The National Heart Foundation of Australia.

www.stroke.org.uk
UK Stroke Association.

www.strokefoundation.com.au
Australian National Stroke Foundation.

Huntington's Disease

hdlighthouse.org
Independently maintained document site for HD.

home.vicnet.net.au/~ahda
Australian Huntington's Disease Association.

www.hda.org.uk
UK's Huntington's Disease Association Online.

www.hdac.org
US Huntington's Disease Advocacy Center.

www.hdfoundation.org
US-based Hereditary Disease Foundation, which focuses on Huntington's Disease.

www.hdsa.org
Huntington's Disease Society of America.

www.hsc-ca.org
The Huntington's Society of Canada.

www.huntington-assoc.com
International Huntington's Disease Association.

www.huntington-study-group.org
Clinical research group from US, Canada, Europe and Australia.

www.lib.uchicago.edu/~rd13/hd
Personally maintained library of HD-relevant links from US.

www.voyager.co.nz/~huntnz
HD resources in New Zealand.

Mental health

mentalhelp.net
US guide to mental health, psychology and psychiatry sites.

www.mentalhealth.com
Mental health links.

www.mentalhealth.org.nz
Mental Health Foundation of New Zealand.

www.mhc.govt.nz
Mental Health Commission of the New Zealand government.

www.mhe-sme.org
Mental Health Europe.

www.mind.org.uk
Mind, the leading mental health charity in England and Wales.

www.nimh.nih.gov
US government National Institute of Mental Health.

www.nmha.org
US National Mental Health Association.

www.sane.org
Sane Australia, the national charity helping people with mental illness.

Migraine and headaches

www.achenet.org
American Council for Headache Education.

www.headaches.org
National Headache Foundation of US.

www.migraine.ca
The Migraine Association of Canada.

www.migraine.co.nz
New Zealand Migraine Sufferers Support Group.

www.migraine.org.uk
Migraine Action Association, formerly the British Migraine Association.

www.migrainepage.com
Personal Webpage of a migraine sufferer.

Multiple sclerosis

www.ifmss.org.uk
The International Federation of Multiple Sclerosis Societies.

www.msaustralia.org.au
Resources for MS sufferers in Australia.

www.mssocietynz.co.nz
The National Multiple Sclerosis Society of New Zealand.

www.nationalmssociety.org
US National Multiple Sclerosis Society.

Parkinson's Disease

apdaparkinson.com
American Parkinson's Disease Association.

parkinsonsaction.org
US-based Parkinson's Action Network.

webnz.com/parkinsons
The Parkinsonism Society of New Zealand.

www.michaeljfox.org
Actor Michael J. Fox's Foundation for Parkinson's Research.

www.parkinson.ca
The Parkinson Society Canada.

www.parkinson.org
US-based National Parkinson Foundation.

www.parkinsonalliance.net
US Parkinson's Disease research charity.

www.parkinsons.org.au
Parkinson's Australia, formerly the National Australian
Parkinson's Association.

www.parkinsons.org.uk
UK Parkinson's Disease Society.

www.parkinsonsdisease.com
Awakenings, an open forum about Parkinson's Disease.

www.pdindex.com
A directory of Parkinson's Disease information.

www.wpda.org
World Parkinson's Disease Association.

Other

www.amdalliance.org
The Age-related Macular Degeneration International Alliance
provides information about the primary cause of blindness in
people over fifty in the West.

www.britishdeafassociation.org.uk
The British Deaf Association.

www.continence-foundation.org.uk
The UK Continence Foundation.

www.eyecare-information-service.org.uk
The UK Eyecare Trust.

www.meningitis-trust.org.uk
The Meningitis Trust, UK.

WOMEN'S HEALTH

thriveonline.oxygen.com
Well-designed women's health portal.

www.akhealth.co.nz/nwhealthinfo
New Zealand National Women's Hospital.

www.awhn.org.au
Australian Women's Health Network.

www.cwhn.ca
Canadian Women's Health Network.

www.fwhc.org
US Feminist Women's Health Center.

www.healthywomen.org
US National Women's Health Resource Center.

www.womens-health.co.uk
Women's Health Information from the UK.

www.womens-health.com
Women's Health Interactive from US.

www.womens-health.org.nz
Women's Health Trust from New Zealand.

www.womenshealthmatters.ca
Women's Health Matters Network from Canada.

Links: Women
    Environmental Issues and World Concerns/AIDS
    Environmental Issues and World Concerns/Drugs
    Environmental Issues and World Concerns/Elderly
     and Ageing

History and Archaeology

Embracing probably the biggest subject possible, sites related to history are manifold on the Web. Here are a few of our favourites.

HISTORY

www.channel4.com/blackhistorymap
Black and Asian history map from the UK's Channel 4 television channel.**ⓕ**

www.coldwar.org
Website of the nomadic Cold War Museum which exhibits around the world.

www.forgottenhistory.org
Site aiming to keep under-documented histories alive.

www.frontiertrails.com
US frontier history, featuring ghost towns and the old west.

www.ghosttowns.com
More ghost towns and the history of the American West. Beware the midi hoe-down.

www.historytoday.com
Online presence of the leading UK history journal, published for over 50 years.

www.holocaustmemorialday.gov.uk
UK government site promoting January 27 as Holocaust Memorial Day.

www.scran.ac.uk
Accessing history and culture through one million images, movies, sounds and virtual reality records.

www.wall-berlin.org
Online exhibition commemorating the tenth anniversary of the fall of the Berlin Wall from Berlin's German History Museum.

www.worldwar1.com
Independent site about the horrors of World War I.

ARCHAEOLOGY AND THE ANCIENT WORLD

Archaeology encompasses virtually the whole history of mankind, from prehistory to medieval times. Here's a small selection of archaeological and ancient world Websites.

argos.evansville.edu
Argos, the Ancient and Medieval limited area search engine, whose results are certified by an editorial board.

www.archaeology.co.uk
The Website of *Current Archaeology*, the popular UK magazine, includes a directory of over 900 archaeological organisations. ⑤

www.archaeology.org
Magazine from the Archaeological Institute of America.

www.britarch.ac.uk
The Council for British Archaeology works to promote the study and safeguarding of Britain's historic environment.

www.culture.fr/culture/arcnat/lascaux/en
Digitally explore the caves of Lascaux.

www.digital-documents.co.uk
Popular Archaeology is the home of a fully searchable database of over 40,000 UK archaeological sites.

www.julen.net/ancient
The Ancient World Web Directory.

Humour, Weird and Bizarre

There's a lot of humour, weirdness and general bizarreness on the Web. Much of it is of an adult nature. Here are some of the sites we particularly liked.

HUMOUR

www.cartoonscape.com
Cartoons, comics and animation.

www.comedy-zone.net
Independently run, professional looking site from the UK with links to stand-up comedian sites and comedy venues.

www.comicasylum.co.uk
Weird comics.

www.dilbert.com
The official Dilbert website.

www.theonion.com
No subject is untouchable for America's alternative news source.❺

WEIRD AND BIZARRE

uglypeople.com
Politically incorrect mugshots.

weirdlinks.com
All the weirdness anyone could handle.

www.disobey.com
Strange ramblings that seem to have something to say.

www.disobey.com/ghostsites
The Museum of E-Failure, where doomed Net ventures reside.

www.disturbingauctions.com
'Sometimes trash is just trash'. Check the attic now.

www.e-sheep.com
Adult comics.

www.faecesoftheworld.co.uk
Distorted celebrity, royalty and politician portraits. **F**

www.netauthority.org
Policing the Web?

www.pixyland.org/peterpan
Vaguely amusing camp nonsense.

www.uglycars.co.uk
The ugliest cars in Britain.

www.virtualfoodfight.com
Food fights by e-mail.

www.whatshouldiputonthefence.com
Like being inside someone else's head.

www.zompist.com
Beyond description.

Kids

We've all heard the stories about kids being able to use the Internet better than their parents, and they're probably true. To the younger generation the Internet is just another part of life, rather than being one of the latest challenging technological developments as it is to many adults, and they generally take to it like ducks to water. In the coming years this will fuel the growth of the Internet as Net-aware kids turn into Net-enabled adults.

As in the big wide world as a whole, there are dangers on the Net from which responsible parents wish to protect their offspring, and there are a number of software filter packages that have evolved to make unsavoury content inaccessible. Details of these can be found in the WebStuff section of this book. Also, on the basis that parents will pay to protect what is dearest to them, a number of subscriber services have evolved which purport to limit what kids can access.

There are sites aimed at kids of all ages, from the youngest to teens, and the content changes accordingly. Homework and general education sites aimed at kids are particularly prevalent. Some of the most entertaining sites are built around the popular kids' characters from comics, books and television. Many of the sites aimed at kids are colourful Flash-driven sites, so the faster your connection the better.

UNITED KINGDOM

harrypotter.warnerbros.co.uk
The Harry Potter industry's official online presence.

kotn.ntu.ac.uk
Kids on the Net encourages writing in children from 6 to 16. **F**

www.artkids.co.uk
Classy creative digital art activity site. **F**

www.atkidz.com
This lively site includes homework help.

www.bbc.co.uk/littlekids
Fireman Sam, Bob the Builder, Postman Pat and other favourite children's television characters can be found at the BBC's site for the under 6s.

www.blyton.com
Noddy and Big Ears, the Famous Five and the Secret Seven from Enid Blyton.

www.bobthebuilder.com
Bob's own site.

www.cool-reads.co.uk
Book reviews by and for 10–15 year olds.

www.foxkids.co.uk
Colourful UK kids' site with lots of animation.

www.funwithspot.com
Excellent and well-crafted interactive games and activity site with Spot the Dog. ❻

www.kids-channel.co.uk
Colouring corner, stories and games at this flashy site.

www.kidzunited.com
Football fun and games for Kidz.

www.mrsmad.com
Children's books reviewed at Mrs Mad's Book-a-Rama.

www.peterrabbit.co.uk
Lavishly illustrated international site from *The World of Peter Rabbit and Friends* by Beatrix Potter.

www.thomasthetankengine.com
From the golden days of rail travel.

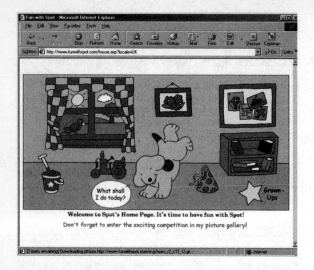

www.thunderbirdsonline.com
Calling International Rescue...

www.tintin.com/uk
Wonderful animation in Hergé's *Adventures of Tintin and Snowy* (Or is it Milou?). ❻

www.ukfavouritesforkids.com
Hand-built search directory aimed at kids from 3 to 14.

www.winniethepooh.co.uk
Winnie the Pooh and Tigger too.

UNITED STATES

alfy.lycos.com
Colourful kids site from Lycos.

cybersleuth-kids.com
Directory search homework help.

thesimpsons.com
Bart and family entertain kids and adults alike.

www.brainpop.com
Health, science and technology education site.

www.eduhound.com
Educational Websites.

www.highlightsforchildren.com
Subscription service to US children's magazine, *Highlights*, which from humble beginnings in 1946 now has a print subscription of 2.5 million.

www.kidlink.org
Multi-language global friends network for kids.

www.kids.gov
US government kids portal.

www.kidsclick.org
Searchable librarian-created directory of over 600 subject headings that guides to good sites, rather than prohibiting unacceptable content.

www.kids-space.org
Using the Internet to enable kids to communicate internationally.

www.magicalharrypotter.com
US Harry Potter fan site.

www.muppets.com
Kermit and Miss Piggy live.

www.netparents.com
Big page of links to kids sites.

www.randomhouse.com/seussville
Dr Seuss and friends, including the *Cat in the Hat*.

www.sesameworkshop.org
All your favourites from *Sesame Street*.

www.starwars.com
The official site.

www.surfmonkey.com
Good looking premium kids' browser site that promises safe chat and clean surfing, but at a price.

www.surfnetkids.com
Newspaper columnist's choice of sites for kids.

www.yahooligans.com
Yahoo! directory for kids.

www.yucky-kids.discovery.com
Messy fun with Wendell the worm.

Links: WebStuff/Filters, Blocks and Washers

Music

MP3, the audio file format, is one of the most commonly searched terms on the Web. Much of the media attention given to the Internet focuses on the ongoing battle between the recording industry and companies such as Napster who facilitate file sharing between Internet users. The legal tussle continues, and Napster has been neutered, but there are still many ways to exchange music files.

Music also appears on the Web in the guise of streaming Web-radio, which is covered in the Radio and Television section. Not surprisingly, you will need a sound card and a media player to listen to music, plus a set of speakers or headphones.

CD reviews and sales outlets are plentiful on the Web, together with the review magazines that pick the best of recorded music. As well as the mainstream rock-pop-oriented music that dominates the charts, there are sites dedicated to virtually all other types of music. Classical music has a strong presence, and you can follow the concert schedules of orchestras and opera companies. Many of the major artists, whatever their musical style, have Websites.

GENERAL MUSIC INFORMATION

www.allmusic.com
All styles of music introduced and explained.

www.musicomh.com
This UK-based overview site covers music generally, with CD and concert reviews for both mainstream acts and opera.

Music magazines
www.billboard.com
www.nme.com
www.rollingstone.com
www.q4music.com

CLASSICAL MUSIC

Classical music is well represented on the Web. Most major orchestras have Websites with programme and season information.

General information

www.choirs.org.uk
Links to UK choral Websites.

www.classical.net
Classical CD reviews and classical music links.

www.classicstoday.com
Classical recordings reviewed.

www.naxos.com
Informative site of the Naxos label.

Orchestras

WORLDWIDE

www.orchestranet.co.uk
Includes UK symphony and chamber orchestra directory, and other orchestras worldwide.

NATIONAL
Australia

www.aso.com.au
Adelaide Symphony Orchestra.

www.mso.com.au
Melbourne Symphony Orchestra.

www.qso.com.au
Queensland Orchestra.

www.symphony.org.au
Sydney Symphony Orchestra.

www.waso.com.au
West Australian Symphony Orchestra.

Canada

www.osm.ca
Montreal Symphony Orchestra.

www.tso.on.ca
Toronto Symphony Orchestra.

www.vancouversymphony.ca
Vancouver Symphony Orchestra.

New Zealand

www.nzso.co.uk
New Zealand Symphony Orchestra.

United Kingdom

www.bbc.co.uk/orchestras
Links to pages for the BBC National Orchestra of Wales, BBC Scottish Symphony Orchestra, BBC Philharmonic, BBC Concert Orchestra and the BBC Symphony Orchestra.

www.cbso.co.uk
City of Birmingham Symphony Orchestra.

www.londonsinfonietta.org.uk
London Sinfonietta.

www.lpo.org.uk
London Philharmonic Orchestra.

www.lso.co.uk
London Symphony Orchestra.

www.philharmonia.co.uk
Philharmonia Orchestra, resident at London's Royal Festival Hall.

www.rlps.co.uk
Royal Liverpool Philharmonic Orchestra.

www.rpo.co.uk
Royal Philharmonic Orchestra.

www.rsno.org.uk
Royal Scottish National Orchestra.

United States

kennedy-center.org/nso
National Symphony Orchestra.

www.atlantasymphony.org
Atlanta Symphony Orchestra.

www.baltimoresymphony.org
Baltimore Symphony Orchestra.

www.bso.org
Boston Symphony Orchestra.

www.cincinnatisymphony.org
Cincinnati Symphony Orchestra.

www.clevelandorch.com
Cleveland Orchestra.

www.cso.org
Chicago Symphony Orchestra.

www.dallassymphony.com
Dallas Symphony Orchestra.

www.grsymphony.org
Grand Rapids Symphony Orchestra.

www.houstonsymphony.org
Houston Symphony Orchestra.

www.indyorch.org
Indianapolis Symphony Orchestra.

www.laphil.org
Los Angeles Philharmonic Orchestra.

www.lpomusic.com
Louisiana Philharmonic Orchestra.

www.lyricopera.org
Lyric Opera of Chicago.

www.milwaukeesymphony.org
Milwaukee Symphony Orchestra.

www.minnesotaorchestra.org
Minnesota Orchestra.

www.nyphilharmon.org
New York Phiharmonic Orchestra.

www.orsymphony.org
Oregon Symphony Orchestra.

www.philorch.org
Philadelphia Orchestra.

www.pittsburghsymphony.org
Pittsburgh Symphony Orchestra.

www.sasymphony.org
San Antonio Symphony Orchestra.

www.seattlesymphony.org
Seattle Symphony Orchestra.

www.sfsymphony.org
San Francisco Symphony Orchestra.

www.slso.org
Saint Louis Symphony Orchestra.

OPERA

General information

theoperacritic.com
An excellent opera links site, from New Zealand.**⑤**

www.fsz.bme.hu/opera/companies.html
Page of worldwide opera company links.

www.opera.co.uk
Opera magazine from the UK.

www.operabase.com
Excellent opera resource, including reviews from around the world, audio and video recordings, performance archives and over a thousand links.**⑤**

www.operalinks.com
Links to opera sites, events and singers.

www.operaworld.com
Opera education and resource centre.

National

AUSTRALIA

www.opera-australia.org.au
Opera Australia.

www.soh.nsw.gov.au
Sydney Opera House.

CANADA

www.coc.ca
Canadian Opera Company.

NEW ZEALAND

www.nzopera.com
New Zealand Opera.

UNITED KINGDOM

www.eno.org
English National Opera.

www.glyndebourne.com
Glyndebourne Festival and Touring Opera.

www.roh.org.uk
Royal Opera House.

www.scottishopera.org.uk
Scottish Opera.

UNITED STATES

www.laopera.org
Los Angeles Opera.

www.metopera.org
Metropolitan Opera.

www.nycopera.com
New York City Opera.

www.sdopera.com
San Diego Opera.

www.sfopera.com
San Francisco Opera.

International opera

A selection of international opera houses.

FRANCE

www.opera-de-paris.fr
French National Opera, Paris.

GERMANY

www.bayerische.staatsoper.de
Bavarian State Opera and Ballet, Munich.

www.deutsche-oper.berlin.de
Deutsche Oper, Berlin.

www.komische-oper-berlin.de
Komische Oper, Berlin.

www.staatsoper-berlin.org
German State Opera, Berlin.

ITALY

www.teatroallascala.org
The Scala, Milan.

SPAIN

www.liceubarcelona.com
Liceu, Barcelona.

JAZZ

wwww.allaboutjazz.com
www.bbc.co.uk/music/styles/jazz.shtml
www.harlem.org
www.jazzcanadiana.on.ca
www.jazzcorner.com❻
www.jazzhall.org
www.jazzonln.com
www.jazzreview.com
www.pbs.org/jazz
www.redhotjazz.com
www.satchmo.com

OTHER MUSIC

Good starting points from which to explore the vast array of
music on the Web not covered in depth in other sections.

www.breakbeat.co.uk
Drum and Bass.

www.danceportal.co.uk
Global Dance.

www.darkerthanblue.com
Rap, Hip Hop, R 'n' B, Reggae, UK Garage.

www.niceup.com
Reggae links.

www.theiceberg.com
Links music under the surface.

www.worldmusicportal.com
Impressive site of world music information and links.**ⓕ**

ARTISTS

It is now fairly common for a Website to be established by record industry companies to accompany individual albums, providing sample tracks or clips of tracks, photos and background information about the making of the album – a kind of intelligent advertisement.

Artists in the main have been slower than might have been expected to create their own official Websites, although many are now established and provide information regarding new releases and forthcoming tour dates. For every official site there are a multitude of unofficial fan sites, many of which contain excellent information.

Listed below are what we believe are official sites from a selection of artists.

Classical and minimalist

www.janeeaglen.com
www.gavinbryars.com
www.michaelnyman.com
www.philipglass.com
www.ravishankar.org
www.stockhausen.org

Rock and pop

bobdylan.com
www.blur.co.uk
www.davidbowie.com
www.dead.net
www.eltonjohn.com
www.officialjanis.com
www.loureed.com
www.stones.com
www.u2.com❶

Album sites

www.forthestars.net
www.nickcave.net
www.thebeatles.com

FILE SHARING AND DOWNLOADS

The long-running debate over the legality of music file-sharing over the Internet continues, but there's still plenty of music out there, from both established bands and artists, and musical hopefuls.

www.angrycoffee.com
www.emusic.com
www.gnutella.co.uk
www.imesh.com
www.launch.com
www.listen.com
www.mp3.com
www.mp3.lycos.com
www.mp3place.com
www.mp3sound.com
www.musicnet.com
www.napster.com
www.peoplesound.com

www.pressplay.com
www.seekmp3.com
www.vitaminic.co.uk
www.webnoize.com
www.zeropaid.com

MEDIA PLAYERS

You'll need a media player in order to listen to music files or radio over the Internet, and to watch streaming Webcasts and on-demand video. There are many media players; however, the most popular are Windows Media Player from Microsoft, RealPlayer from RealNetworks and QuickTime from Apple.

www.apple.com/quicktime
Details of QuickTime products.

www.microsoft.com/windows/windowsmedia
Information about the different versions of Windows Media Player and downloads.

www.real.com
Details of the full range of RealNetworks products.

Links: Radio and Television/Radio

Nature

The natural world is well catered for by the Web, with sites dedicated to specific bird and animal species, as well as information sites run by zoos and aquaria. The animal protection sites can be particularly good ways of finding out more about particular groups of animals.

ANIMAL INFORMATION

abcissa.co.uk/birds
Independent bird-lovers' site from the UK, showing birds in a Cheshire garden.

allaboutfrogs.org
Silly cartoon frogs.

www.africam.com
Observe wildlife in its natural habitat worldwide with WebCams. ⓕ

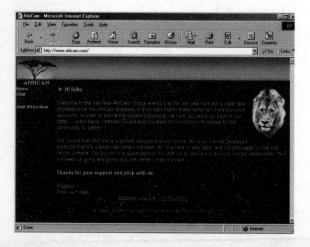

www.hummingbirds.net
Interesting facts about North American Hummingbirds.

www.wildnetafrica.com
African wildlife information portal.

www.zoo-keeper.co.uk
Informative animal index.

ANIMAL PROTECTION AGENCIES

savethekoala.com
Australia Koala Foundation.

www.awf.org
The African Wildlife Federation has worked to conserve wildlife for over forty years.

www.bats.org.uk
UK Bat Conservation Trust.

www.bornfree.org.uk
Dedicated to preserving species in their natural habitat and the phasing out of traditional zoos.**F**

www.cats.org.uk
UK Cats Protection League.

www.cfhs.ca
The Canadian Federation of Humane Societies provides animal welfare information for Canada.

www.ewt.org.za
The Endangered Wildlife Trust of South Africa.

www.ifaw.org
US-based International Fund for Animal Welfare.

www.pdsa.org.uk
People's Dispensary for Sick Animals, 'for pets in need of vets'.

www.rspb.org.uk
UK's Royal Society for the Protection of Birds.

www.rspca.org.uk
UK's Royal Society for the Prevention of Cruelty to Animals.

www.wag.co.za
Wildlife Action Group of South Africa.

www.wdcs.org
The Whale and Dolphin Conservation Society.

www.wildlifetrusts.org
The Wildlife Trusts partnership is the UK's leading
conservation charity exclusively dedicated to wildlife.

www.wspa.org.uk
World Society for the Protection of Animals.

www.wwf.org
Links to international sites of the World Wildlife Fund Global
Network, campaigning for over forty years, including:

www.panda.org	International
www.wwf.org.au	Australian
www.wwfcanada.org	Canada
www.wwf.org.nz	New Zealand
www.panda.org.za	South Africa
www.wwf.org.uk	United Kingdom
www.wwfus.org	United States

www.zoocheck.com
Canadian national animal protection charity established to
protect wildlife in captivity and in the wild.

Links: Environmental Issues and World Concerns/
Environment and Ecology

AQUARIA AND ZOOS

The question mark over zoos doesn't go away: do they represent the cruel and unnatural incarceration of animals for human amusement? Or are they reputable educational institutions for the study, preservation and conservation of endangered species? This selection of zoological sites may shed some light on this taxing issue.

Worldwide

ammpa.org
Educational resource from the international Alliance of Marine Mammals and Aquariums.

www.aqualink.com/community/publicaquariums.html
Referenced list and links to public aquaria around the world.

www.goodzoos.com
Good Zoo Guide to zoos, wildlife parks and animal collections.

www.zoos-worldwide.com
Zoos information, news and site directory.

www.zooweb.net
US-based site listing zoos and aquaria from around the world.**ⓕ**

Australia

aquarium.gbrmpa.gov.au
The great barrier reef aquarium.

www.arazpa.org.au
Australasian Regional Association of Zoological Parks and Aquaria.

www.sydneyaquarium.com.au
Sydney's world-class aquarium.

Canada

www.caza.ca
Canadian Association of Zoos and Aquariums.

www.marinelandcanada.com
Marineland theme park, Niagara Falls.

www.vanaqua.org
Vancouver Aquarium Marine Science Centre.

New Zealand

www.aucklandzoo.co.nz
Auckland Zoo information site.

South Africa

www.aquarium.co.za
The Two-Oceans aquarium, Cape Town.

www.paazab.org
Pan-African Association of Zoological Gardens, Aquaria and Botanic Gardens.

United Kingdom

www.aquariauk.com
Comprehensive directory of public aquaria in the UK.**ⓕ**

www.edinburghzoo.org.uk
Edinburgh Zoo, Scotland.

www.londonaquarium.co.uk
The London Aquarium, South Bank.

www.londonzoo.co.uk
Zoological Society of London at London Zoo.

www.longleat.co.uk
Wildlife safari park at Longleat, UK.

United States

wcs.org
New York's Wildlife Conservation Society at the Bronx Zoo.

www.aqua.org
The National Aquarium, Baltimore.

www.aquariums.state.nc.us
North Carolina aquariums.

www.aza.org
Directory of the American Zoo and Aquarium Association,
searchable by state.

www.mbayaq.org
Monterey Bay aquarium.

www.neaq.org
The New England Aquarium, Boston.

www.seattleaquarium.org
The Seattle Aquarium.

Links: Gardening/Botanical Gardens and Arboreta

News

The provision of news is perfectly suited to the immediacy of the Web. Anyone hooked-up and logged-on can receive news as soon as it happens, quicker than ever before. Many users keep a news window on their computer terminal to ensure that they are always informed. Every type of news is catered for, including business, sport, finance, and current affairs.

News sites can combine the best of radio and newspapers, providing both speed and in-depth analysis for breaking news. The recent appalling World Trade Center disaster indicated the level to which the Web is now regarded by many as an effective source of news, with news sites being inundated within minutes of the event by people trying to find information, temporarily paralysing the servers.

Broadcast and print media overlap on the Web as broadcasters and newspapers vie with each other to be the news supplier of choice. Most newspapers now have Websites and the best are highly impressive. Many offer searchable archives which can be invaluable research resources.

Some news sites incorporate video clips, but there seems little point in using the standard talking head, although some channels do offer this. The conditions under which viewers watch clips is not particularly good, and for most news, audio or text-based material would seem to do the job just as well. To get around this problem, a number of news-provision organisations have attempted to make presenter-fronted news a form of info-tainment, such as Ananova's animated newsreader. In practice, however, such tactics have only short-term appeal, as the novelty soon wears thin.

The addition of video clips is most effective when there is a news item of great importance that can be represented in summary by moving images. The most apparent instances of this are disasters, where the images rapidly take on iconic status. Examples are the Concorde air crash in 2000 and the World Trade Center disaster of 2001.

As is often the case with the Web, it's the old ideas, digitally reconstituted, that often work best. News tickers, the scrolling headline boxes that appear in many sites, have their roots in the nineteenth century, when stock quotations were first received telegraphically, and in newswires. It's now standard practice for tickers to be provided within general portal sites such as msn.com. Some Internet users incorporate a ticker feed into their system so that it is always on-screen, providing instant access to the headlines.

Another concept into which new life has been breathed is the standard newspaper layout, with its layering of headline, summary line and then main body text. In digital news practice, rather than coexisting on a single page of a newspaper, these constituent elements of news communication are layered across linked pages. The reader clicks on the headlines, perhaps from a ticker, and is sent to a news item page, where a summary article is available. There additional links are provided that can be clicked on in any order to flesh out the story further. In terms of structure, readers are in control of how they consume the news.

What readers do not control, of course, is the content of the news. Decisions as to which items reach the status of 'news' and the extent to which details are made public is key to the news management process. Simultaneously and paradoxically, while there is an ever-proliferating and potentially overwhelming number of possible news sources, via the multiplied outlets of satellite and cable television as well as the Web, they all seem to recycle the same stories and angles on any particular news item.

Items of news are fed into the media machine by a powerful breed of news controllers in the form of lobbyists, PR agencies and other communications specialists, all with vested interests. The need for speed in news delivery means that sorting out the 'facts' behind a story often takes second place to releasing it, making news provision companies vulnerable to spin from governments and commercial concerns. The 'breaking news' syndrome means that there is often little time to verify or dig deeper into stories.

Increasingly feeling subject to a form of state and corporate-controlled media propaganda, some news consumers are gradually turning to the burgeoning alternative media sources available on the Web. Their self-professed aims of reaching the 'truth' and reading around, behind and between the lines of the mainstream news stories are reflected in their increasing popularity and profile.

Investigative journalism, for a time seemingly verging on extinction as it was squeezed from the pages of mainstream publications, has been resurrected, resurfacing on the alternative news portals and journals. Writers taking a stance outside and sometimes actively opposed to the mainstream have a growing number of platforms on the Web from which to proffer their views.

GENERAL NEWS SITES

www.abyznewslinks.com
Global directory-style link site to newspapers, news media and news sources.

www.alertnet.org
Global international news, communications and logistics service for the public and disaster relief organisations from the Reuters Foundation, an educational and humanitarian trust. **ⓕ**

www.indymedia.org
An alternative approach to media coverage is offered by this collective of independent media organisations and hundreds of journalists worldwide which aim to provide information without corporate influence, and aspire to report the 'truth'. **ⓕ**

www.insideworld.com
News portal providing top stories selected by geographical region, with optional daily e-mail news service.**ⓕ**

www.irn.co.uk
Independent Radio News supplies radio news bulletins to 240 national, regional and local UK radio stations. You can listen to the latest bulletin at this site.

www.kidon.com/media-link
Independent directory of newspapers and other Internet news sources, arranged by region.

www.mediachannel.org
A non-profit public interest Website dedicated to global media issues. Aiming to provide diverse perspective and information, MediaChannel is concerned with the political, cultural and social impacts of the media, and sifts information provided by hundreds of organisations worldwide.

www.newsaide.com
Headline news sorted into 18 categories and over 330 subcategories.

www.newsdirectory.com
Directory links to newspapers, magazines, television stations, colleges, visitor bureaux and government agencies.

www.newsrack.com
Searchable database of online newspapers and magazines from the Menzies groups.

www.newstrawler.com
International News Search Engine.

www.tol.cz
Covering twenty-eight countries in central and eastern Europe, Prague-based Transitions OnLine provides unique cross-regional analysis.**ⓕ**

Other general news sites

www.1stheadlines.com
www.newsblip.com
www.newsindex.com
www.rapidtree.com
www.totalnews.com
www.wnnetwork.com

NATIONAL NEWS SITES
Australia

www.abc.net.au/news
www.australiadaily.com
www.news.com.au
www.skynews.com.au

Canada

ca.dailynews.yahoo.com
cbc.ca/newsworld
www.canada.com/news

NEWSWIRE AND PRESS AGENCIES

www.cdn-news.com
www.cp.org
www.newscanada.com
www.newswire.ca

New Zealand

onenews.nzoom.com
xtramsn.co.nz/news
www.newsroom.co.nz
www.scoop.co.nz
www.stuff.co.nz

South Africa

allafrica.com

news.24.com
www.iol.co.za

NEWSWIRE AND PRESS AGENCIES

www.woza.co.za

United Kingdom

news.bbc.co.uk
portal.telegraph.co.uk
www.ananova.com
www.channel4news.co.uk
www.itn.co.uk
www.newsnow.co.uk🄵
www.scotsman.com
www.skynews.co.uk
www.teletext.co.uk

NEWSWIRE AND PRESS AGENCIES

www.pa.press.net
www.reuters.com

United States

abcnews.go.com
www.7am.com🄵
www.cnn.com
www.foxnews.com
www.newsday.com

NEWSWIRE AND PRESS AGENCIES

www.ap.org

NEWSPAPERS

Newspaper link sites

www.thatsnewstome.com
Link portal to newspapers, news sources, plus thousands of
magazines worldwide.

www.thepaperboy.com
An excellent site that has links to virtually all the many thousands
of newspaper sites worldwide. **❺**

National newspapers

AUSTRALIA

afr.com
Australian Financial Review.

canberra.yourguide.com.au
The Canberra Times.

www.smh.com.au
The Sydney Morning Herald.

www.theage.com.au
The Melbourne Age.

www.theaustralian.news.com.au

CANADA

www.canada.com/calgary/calgaryherald
www.canada.com/edmonton/edmontonjournal
www.canada.com/montreal/montrealgazette
www.canada.com/vancouver/vancouversun
www.globeandmail.ca
www.nationalpost.com
www.thestar.com

NEW ZEALAND

www.nzherald.co.nz

SOUTH AFRICA

www.iol.co.za/html/frame_thestar.php
The Star.

www.mg.co.za
Daily Mail and Guardian.

www.sundaytimes.co.za

UNITED KINGDOM
www.belfasttelegraph.co.uk

www.dailytelegraph.co.uk
The Daily and *Sunday Telegraph.*

www.express.co.uk
Daily and *Sunday Express.*

www.ft.com
The Financial Times.

www.independent.co.uk

www.observer.co.uk
Hosted by Guardian Unlimited.

www.mirror.co.uk
www.muslimnews.co.uk
www.newsoftheworld.co.uk
www.scotlandonsunday.com

www.sundaymail.co.uk
Scottish Sunday Mail.

www.theherald.co.uk
The Glasgow Herald.

www.thescotsman.co.uk
www.thesun.co.uk
www.thetimes.co.uk

www.thisislondon.co.uk
London Evening Standard.

UNITED STATES

public.wsj.com
The Wall Street Journal.

www.boston.com/globe
The Boston Globe.

www.chicagotribune.com

www.iht.com
International Herald Tribune.

www.latimes.com
Los Angeles Times.

www.newyorktimes.com

www.nypost.com
The New York Post.

www.usatoday.com
www.washingtonpost.com

www.washtimes.com
The Washington Times.

EUROPEAN NEWSPAPER SITES

Belgium
www.standaard.be

Finland
www.aamulehti.fi

France
www.lemonde.fr
www.leparisien.fr
www.liberation.fr

Germany

morgenpost.berlin1.de
Berliner Morgenpost.

www.faz.de
Frankfurter Allgemeine.

www.welt.de
Die Welt.

Greece

www.ethnos.gr

Ireland

www.ireland.com
The Irish Times.

www.unison.ie/irish_independent
The Irish Independent.

Italy

www.corriere.it
Corriere della Sera.

www.repubblica.it
La Repubblica.

Netherlands

www.nrc.nl
NCR Handelsblad.

www.telegraaf.nl
www.volkskrant.nl

Norway

www.aftenposten.no

Poland
www.gazeta.pl/alfa/home.jsp

Portugal
www.expresso.pt

Russia
www.moscowtimes.ru
The Moscow Times (in English).

pravda.ru

www.sptimes.ru
The St Petersburg Times (in English).

Spain
www.elmundo.es
www.elpais.es

Sweden
www.expressen.se

Switzerland
www.nzz.ch
Neue Zürcher Zeitung.

Turkey
www.radikal.com.tr

ALTERNATIVE NEWS AND VIEWS

bsd.mojones.com
Non-profit magazine *Mother Jones*, published for over 25 years, is renowned for its investigative journalism.

emperors-clothes.com
Provocative and thought-provoking political and current affairs commentary.

www.alternet.org

Providing visibility to the measured alternative view.**❻**

www.counterpunch.org

Extremely readable alternative takes on political realities from respected columnists.**❻**

www.dissentmagazine.org

Quarterly magazine of politics and culture.

www.fair.org

Fairness and Accuracy in Reporting scrutinises US media practices that marginalise public interest, minority and dissenting viewpoints.

www.freespeech.org
Free Speech Television from US, an alternative to establishment media.🄵

www.indypress.org
US Independent Press Association.🄵

www.inthesetimes.com
US news magazine with an alternative view, committed to extending political and economic democracy.

Links: Arts/Literary and cultural commentary
  Environmental Issues and World Concerns/Freedom
    of Speech and Censorship

People Finding

There are many routes to locating people over the Net, ranging from e-mail directories to telephone number searches. Searches within directories and portals such as Lycos and Yahoo can yield some interesting results, but they can be a bit hit and miss. If you're looking for general references to an individual, using search engines can also be fruitful.

canada411.sympatico.ca
Postcodes and telephone numbers for Canada.

people.yahoo.com
Yahoo! People Search.

whitepages.lycos.com
Lycos White Pages people search.🄵

wp.superpages.com
US People Pages.

www.192directory.co.uk
Worldwide telephone directory and yellow pages search engine.

www.bigfoot.com
US people finding service.

www.bt.com
The British Telecom site provides a link to online UK Directory enquiries.

www.friendsreunited.co.uk
UK site to put old school and college friends back in contact.

www.locateme.com
This US site uses public records, and driver and voter registrations.

www.phonenumbers.net
International phone numbers, faxes and e-mail addresses.

www.switchboard.com
US White Pages, Yellow Pages and Phonebook.

www.worldemail.com
The grandly titled World Email Directory.

Links: WebStuff/Search Engines

Radio and Television

RADIO

There's radio on the Web and there's Web-radio. Many of the thousands of airwave radio stations around the world are now routed over the Web. They can be found by entering a radio location site, which should point you in the right direction. There are also many independent Web-radio stations that provide a service exclusively over the Internet. These range from fairly professional outfits to lone mavericks. Web-only radio often consists of programmed music of a particular type, for example jazz, country or classical, without any discernible human presence. There are also Web-stations that sound similar to conventional stations with DJs and jingles.

To listen to either type, you'll need a sound card in your computer, and, if you want to listen in any degree of comfort, a pair of speakers or headphones. You'll also need to have downloaded to your computer one or more of the many media players that are available.

Radio location sites

goan.com/radio.html
Links to radio stations worldwide.

internetradiolist.com
Accessible searchable listing of radio stations, with short profiles of selected stations.

radio.yahoo.com
Broad selection of radio links from Yahoo!

realguide.real.com/tuner
Select from 2,500 radio stations with the Real media player.

windowsmedia.com/radiotuner
Many stations can be linked to via the Windows Media Player.

www.radio-locator.com

Links to terrestrial radio stations that have an Internet
presence, either as a Website or broadcasting over the
Web.

www.word2word.com/real.html

Selection of links to non-English language radio.

Radio stations

Here's a small selection from the thousands of stations available.

www.classicfm.com

Listen to the UK's independent classical radio station over
the Net.

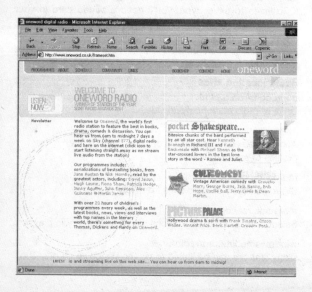

www.oneword.co.uk
Books, drama, comedy and discussion at this impressive talk radio site from London.**F**

www.radiocaroline.co.uk
The radio station that broke the barriers – still alive and still kicking and on the Web.

www.radiofreeworld.com
Web-broadcaster with links to international stations.

www.sonicnet.com
Choice of channels, including Jazz, Latin, Brazilian and Classical, or you can create your own radio station.**F**

www.worldmusicradio.com
Live-hosted Internet-only station, playing traditional and contemporary World Music.

TELEVISION

The proliferation of satellite and cable television channels that sit alongside traditional terrestrial channels means you get a lot more choice on television these days. The vast majority of these channels can't actually be watched over the Internet in the way that radio programmes can be listened to, although some Websites include short video clips. Much of the Web-presence of television is bolstering traditional television. For example, supplementary information about programmes, actors and celebrities, as well as transcripts and archive material, is often provided at network or channel sites. Each channel site also usually carries details of its daily programme schedules.

The much-anticipated implementation of Web-television is faltering somewhat due to the slow roll-out of fast broadband connections to the Internet. These are still out of reach for many users. Domestic users, who are most likely to use Web-television for leisure viewing, are generally the worst served, as even the alleged fast connections that are available to home-based Internet users can be much slower than those provided to businesses.

Business-oriented channels such as Bloomberg, which delivers financial and stocks news, are successfully transmitted over the Net, as corporate Internet users generally have fast connections which can receive flowing visuals, rather than the much delayed and often still or intermittent screen images that dial-up connections deliver.

Worldwide

www.epguides.com
International television programme episode guides.

www.tvradioworld.com
US-based broadcasting industry directory, which includes details of international television and radio channels.

www.tvshow.com
Worldwide information and links relating to television.

National sites

The national television channel sites usually have a homepage covering general mainstream local and world news. Some channel sites, such as the UK's extremely popular BBC Online, have become huge portals that relate to far more than just television content, providing public service information and expanding upon and following-up issues raised by its programmes. Web discussions, chat forums and interviews, and e-mail feedback are means by which viewers can now interact with television channels and programme makers.

AUSTRALIA
General

www.sofcom.com.au/TV
Sofcom provides links to terrestrial, satellite and cable television channel and network sites in Australia, and provides television listings.

Channels

i7.com.au
www.abc.net.au
www.sbs.com.au

CANADA

radio-canada.ca/television
www.cbc.ca
www.ctv.ca

IRELAND

www.rte.ie
Ireland's national broadcasting organisation.

NEW ZEALAND

tv2.nzoom.com
tvone.nzoom.com
www.tv3.co.nz
www.tv4.co.nz

SOUTH AFRICA

www.sabc.co.za
South African Broadcasting Corporation.

UNITED KINGDOM

General

www.cableguide.co.uk
UK cable television listings.

www.digiguide.co.uk
Interactive online television guide for the UK.**❻**

www.itc.org.uk
The Independent Television Commission licenses and
regulates commercially funded television services in the UK.

www.offthetelly.co.uk
Television Criticism with a personal touch.

www.radiotimes.beeb.com
Listings from the *Radio Times*, the UK's long-running radio and television schedules magazine.

www.tv.cream.org
Resurrecting long-dead television programmes.

Channels
www.bbc.co.uk
www.carlton.com
www.channel4.com
www.channel5.co.uk
www.itv.com
www.sky.com

UNITED STATES
General
tv.zap2it.com
US television listings, news and information.

www.gist.com/tv
US Interactive television listings.

www.tvguide.com
Online version of popular television listing magazine.

Channels
abc.go.com
www.bbcamerica.com
www.cbs.com
www.hitn.org
www.nbc.com
www.pbs.org
www.telemundo.com

Television on the Web

Webcasts, including live and on-demand coverage of concerts and newscasts, are now made through a multitude of channels. Huge amounts of video clips are also available from many sources, including movie trailers and music videos. However, there are as yet few established live television channels on the Web.

To receive audio-visual material on the Web you will need a suitably fast broadband connection to the Internet. Audio-only material can be received via standard connections.

The sites listed below represent a taste of what is available:

broadcast.yahoo.com
Yahoo! Broadcast provides a useful explanation of Web broadcasting principles.

broadcast-live.com
Live television and radio broadcasts across the Internet.

wwitv.com
Live worldwide streaming links to national broadcast organisations.❶

www.bloomberg.com/tv
Live Web feeds of Bloomberg's international financial cable and satellite television, including channels for France, Japan, Spain and US.

www.bwebb.co.uk
Clips, trailers, videos and shorts.

www.onlineclassics.com
A selection of on-demand performances of classics from the worlds of theatre, dance, opera and classical music at this excellent performing arts site.❶

Links: Music

Science and Space

Here's our selection from the many science and space sites to be found across the Web.

SCIENCE

www.bbc.co.uk/science
Human Body, Space, Technology, Dinosaurs and Learning sections at BBC Online's Science channel.

www.clifton-scientific.org
The Clifton Scientific Trust is a UK educational charity seeking to encourage student participation in scientific projects which address real problems in the real world.

www.explorescience.com
Science teaching resource.

www.gsc.org.uk
Scotland's millennial flagship project, the Glasgow Science Centre, opened in July 2001 and aims to bring science and technology to life through hundreds of interactive exhibits in the science mall, state-of-the art cinema, and the groundbreaking Glasgow Tower.🅕

www.invent.org
US National Inventors Hall of Fame.

www.jb.man.ac.uk/scicen
The Jodrell Bank Science Centre and Planetarium, Manchester, UK, includes the visitor centre for the Lovell Radio Telescope and the Jodrell Bank Observatory.

www.junkscience.com
Debunking manipulative science myths?

www.newscientist.com
Online version of the essential international magazine that has delivered scientific news since 1956. Informed special

reports on GM crops, mobile phones, BSE, marijuana and other issues of the day.**❻**

www.popsci.com
Popular Science magazine.

www.robotwars.co.uk
Official Website of the televisual cult.

www.rsnz.govt.nz
The Royal Society of New Zealand, promoting and advancing science and technology.

www.scienceagogo.com
Science news with a hint of satire.

www.sciencemag.org
Subscription publication from the American Association for the Advancement of Science.

www.sciencenet.org.uk
Excellent science information service.**❻**

www.sciencenews.org
Online version of the weekly magazine published since 1922, covering important research across all fields of science.

www.treasure-troves.com
Astronomy, chemistry and physics are covered in this accessible encyclopaedic site.

Links: Museums and Galleries/Museums

SPACE AND ASTRONOMY

starryskies.com
Educational atmosphere at this informative tour of the galaxy.

www.bbc.co.uk/science/space
BBC Online's Space Zone, including *The Sky at Night*, one of

the few television programmes to have been broadcast in five different decades.**F**

www.esrin.esa.it
European Space Agency portal.

www.nasa.gov
The US government's National Aeronautics and Space Administration site.

www.nasm.edu
National Air and Space Museum at the Smithsonian Institute, Washington DC.

www.nss.org
A view of life in outer space from the US National Space Society.

www.nssc.co.uk
UK National Space Centre, a visitor attraction with educational and research facilities in Leicestershire, UK.

www.ras.org.uk
Founded in 1820, the UK's Royal Astronomical Society promotes astronomy and geophysics.

www.space.com
Making space fun with space news games, entertainment and science fiction.

www.spacedaily.com
US portal to an intriguing network of space channels.

www.space-frontier.org
Californian-based media and policy organisation working to make space open, dynamic and inclusive.

www.spaceweather.com
Discover whether the sun's out in space.

www.stsci.edu
The Space Telescope Science Institute, Baltimore, is
responsible for operating the Hubble Space Telescope as an
international observatory.

Shopping

There are thousands of shopping sites on the Internet. We feel that these are well serviced by other guides and therefore have chosen not to list general shopping sites here. However, we have selected a few ethical consumer and investment sites for inclusion.

Ethical consumption means buying products and services that benefit the consumer, the producer and the workers, and at the same time don't harm the environment. It's often difficult to find products and services that fulfil these credentials, but a growing awareness of such concerns means that more are becoming available. It's often confusing sorting out which products are green, which are organic, which are natural, and which are considered ethical. The following sites offer some advice and guidance.

FAIR TRADE AND ETHICAL CONSUMERISM

Ethical shopping

greenbabyco.com
Ethically sound baby products.

www.coopamerica.org
US site providing information about using consumer and investor power for social change.

www.eighth-day.co.uk
Manchester-based ethical cooperative.

www.ethicalconsumer.org
Ethical Consumer Research Association.

www.ethicalexchange.co.uk
Ethical news, plus products and services directory.**Ⓕ**

www.ethical-junction.org
Ethical organisation and ethical trading.

www.fairtrade.org.uk
Fairtrade guarantees a better deal for third world producers.

www.fairtradefederation.com
Directory of US wholesalers, retailers and producers
committed to fair wages and good employment opportunities
and work conditions.

www.getethical.com
Ethical shopping from *The Big Issue* and *Red Pepper*
magazine.**ⓕ**

www.greenchoices.org
Celebrity-supported green tips and links site.**ⓕ**

www.greenmarketplace.com
Natural, organic and cruelty free products.

www.oneworld.net/shop
The Oneworld ethical shop.

Other green sites

www.greenpeople.co.uk
www.greenshop.co.uk
www.naturalcollection.com

ETHICAL INVESTMENT AND BANKING

www.co-operativebank.co.uk
The Co-operative Bank.

www.eiris.org
Ethical Investment Research Service.

www.ethicalinvestment.org.uk
The Ethical Investment Association.

www.ethicalinvestments.co.uk
Independent financial advice from Ethical Investments.

www.gaeia.co.uk
Global and Ethical Investment Advice.

www.thencbs.co.uk
The National Centre for Business and Sustainability.

Links: Environmental Issues and World Concerns/
        Globalisation
        Food and Drink
        Gardens and Gardening/Shopping

Silver Surfers, Seniors, Over 50s

With an estimated thirteen million plus adults over the age of 50 having access to the Internet in the US, and over four million in the UK, there are plenty of silver surfers or seniors out there. The numbers are set to grow further still as the early baby boomer generation move into their 50s. Not surprisingly, therefore, especially in the UK and the US, there are now many sites aimed at those who are aged 50 or over, particularly those who are still working and, on paper at least, are affluent and represent significant spending power. Reflecting this, many of the magazine-style portal sites that have come online in the past three years or so tend to be a slightly dubious mix of relevant information and invitations to spend.

It's about as natural to group together everyone in society over 50 years of age as it is to lump together those between, say, the ages of 20 and 50, but that's what many of these sites do. One site below even sets the lower age of its target group at 45. There are a few exceptions, with the occasional site aimed at those over retirement age and above, but clearly there are now many stages to life, not all of which are well catered for by the Web at the moment. Those who are past retirement age and on low incomes, for example, will find fewer sites aimed specifically at them. We hope that this situation will change as more Internet sites are developed.

A recent survey from the UK's Age Concern reports that older users found that the Net stimulated the mind and bridged the generation gap by providing a common experience with younger people. Most older users find that e-mail can bring the benefit of strengthening relationships with family and friends, and many of the sites below draw upon the notion of community that connecting with others interactively over e-mail can bring.

However, there are also heaps of useful information available out there both about and for older people, including education and learning sites which provide the opportunity to pursue previously overlooked interests. Much of the information is of a local or national nature; hence this section is divided by country, but don't let that stop you looking at sites from other places, as there are lots of creative ideas and thoughts, and useful information, that will be of interest to everyone, wherever they are.

AUSTRALIA

u3aonline.edna.edu.au
The online resources of the University of the Third Age provide educational opportunities in the form of short-term courses.

www.aboutseniors.com.au
Useful link site.

www.cota.org.au
The grammatically curious 'Council on the Ageing' (COTA), a nationwide organisation run by and for older Australians, aims to protect and promote the well-being of all older people.

www.multiculturalaustralia.com.au
Reflecting Australia's rich multicultural society, this site is specially designed for senior Australians from culturally and linguistically diverse backgrounds. It provides e-mail, chat and searches in 16 different languages. **F**

www.seniorlink.com.au
Committed to the view that the computer can be a boon to the lives of older people, SeniorLink's site evolved out of their computer training business.

Other sites for seniors from Australia:
www.geriantics.com.au
www.greypath.com.au
www.nationalseniors.com.au

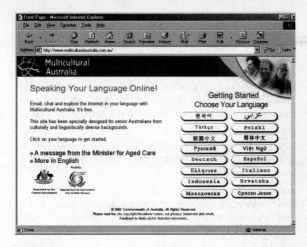

CANADA

fifty-plus.net

The on-line home of CARP, Canada's largest 50+ advocacy group and *CARPNews FiftyPlus* magazine, Canada's popular publication for the over 50s.

UNITED KINGDOM

www.ace.org.uk

Web home of Age Concern, the primary UK charitable movement involved with ageing issues.

www.activage.org.uk

A branch of Age Concern that promotes an active and fulfilling later life by providing new opportunities to those over 50, encouraging them to value their life and work experiences and to share them with others for mutual benefit.

www.bbb.org.uk
The Baby Boomer Bistro was the first chat site in the UK developed specifically for the over 50s. ⑤

www.hairnet.org
A computer and Internet training initiative for the over 50s, which provides a range of options including home visits and retraining for business. The Website hosts a lively interactive club-based community for sharing views and opinions. ⑤

www.hellsgeriatrics.com
Views and opinions with attitude from over 50s who prefer to grow old disgracefully. Fun and seriousness intertwine in this thoughtful site. ⑤

www.housingcare.org
Independent site providing information about housing and care options to enable informed decision making.

www.opin.org.uk
The Old People's Information Network is a well designed, easy-to-use community information resource initiated by Coventry Libraries, which should serve as a model for the rest of the UK. Although primarily aimed at users in the West Midlands, the Directory provides useful information for all. ⑤

www.retirement-matters.co.uk
Useful accessible information and features.

www.seehowtheygrow.com
Bridge the years with this guide for grandparents.

www.silverhairs.co.uk
They don't make them like this anymore. See through the design and layout to reach the useful information and links in these personal help-pages for silver surfers.

www.seniority.co.uk
A fresh, interactive site with a community feel that has been gaining encouraging press in the UK. ⑤

www.theoldie.co.uk
Website promoting *The Oldie*, the informed magazine
established by ex-*Private Eye* editor Richard Ingrams that
helps you grow older with a sense of humour.

www.twilightyears.co.uk
Directory of UK services and information for the elderly.

www.u3a.org.uk
The UK site of the University of the Third Age, which aims to
provide lifelong learning for pleasure and understanding
through over 400 local groups.**Ⓕ**

www.vavo.com
You'll find no references to 'seniors' in this corporate-like
pan-European portal aimed at those over 45.

Other sites aimed at the over 50s from the UK:

www.50connect.co.uk
www.bigfiveoh.com
www.cennet.co.uk
www.idf50.co.uk
www.laterlife.com
www.lifes4living.co.uk
www.maturetymes.co.uk
www.saga.co.uk
www.silversurfers.net
www.thebig50.co.uk
www.thirdagepress.co.uk
www.wiseowls.co.uk
www.wrinklies.org

UNITED STATES

www.2young2retire.com
Thoughtful suggestions for making midlife onwards
enjoyable, fruitful and productive, with personal examples of
alternatives to retirement.**Ⓕ**

www.50plus.org
The Fifty-Plus Fitness Association (FPFA) is a twenty-year-old non-profit organisation whose mission is to promote an active lifestyle for older people.

www.aarp.org
The AARP Foundation provides direct services to senior citizens, particularly in the areas of consumer advocacy, legal assistance, tax counselling, job training and placement, and health care and long-term care information.

www.elderweb.com
This excellent award-winning site has been providing elder and long-term care information since 1994, and now includes over 6,000 links, an expanding library of articles and reports, news, and events. ❺

www.hwsg.com
The Huntsman World Senior Games were established in 1987 for athletes over 50. They take place in Utah annually and now cover 19 sports.

www.seniorlaw.com
US legal advice for seniors, and their advocates and legal professionals.

www.seniornet.com
Award-winning site that promotes and supports the use of computer and communications technologies as a means of enriching the lives of seniors.

www.seniors.gov
Health and security information and services from the official seniors portal of the US government site for the public, first.gov.

www.seniorssearch.com
Search engine and directory that aims to be the portal of choice for those over 50.

www.seniorsww.com
Despite the name, SeniorsWorldwide is a US national
directory providing information state-by-state.

www.thegeezerbrigade.com
'Empowerment through humor!' is the motto of this pay-
subscription site. You've just got to laugh.

www.wiredseniors.com
The hub of the seniors-related sites that compose the
wiredseniors network, including SeniorSearch and Age of
Reason. Provides links to radio stations, discussion forums
and personal ads.

Other US seniors sites:
www.doublenickels.com
www.go60.com
www.grandtimes.com
www.homefrontmagazine.com
www.lovingcare.net
www.retired.com
www.seniors-site.com
www.thirdage.com
www.todaysseniors.com

Links: Environmental Issues and World Concerns/Elderly and
Ageing

Sports

It's not hard to see where the big money lies in sport. The Web highlights the distinction between amateur sports and those sports not yet adopted by the media, and the wealthy top-level professional sports. The highly paid glamour sports of soccer, golf and Formula 1 motor-racing, and to a lesser extent boxing, cricket and rugby union boast a vast number of high quality Websites, while amateur sports sites tend to be run on a shoestring. This is clearly a reflection of the huge fan bases for these big business sports and is a result of the finance jointly invested in high technology development by the ruling bodies, the clubs and media companies.

The close allegiance on the Web of the broadcast media and wealthy professional sports comes as no surprise. Sports content was instrumental in expanding the market for satellite TV, and is doing so for pay-per-view television. It now looks set to do the same for broadband technology with Webcasts. For example, the richest UK soccer clubs are currently redesigning their Websites and making them broadband-friendly, and we can expect to see regular pay-per-view football over the Web soon. As content is king, and the content many people want is immediate online sports coverage, sport looks set to shift porn from its position as the primary Web technology driver.

Other likely future developments within the field of sport on the Web include the availability of online ticketing facilities for sports events and the increased online sale of sports merchandising. Similarly, the syndication of sports results services and video footage across general news sites will become more widespread. It's also likely that sports bodies and clubs will examine ways of bonding further with interested fans by establishing a closer relationship through the provision of statistics, news and history specifically tailorable to the interests of the individual fan.

There are an impressive number of Web-based sports networks, such as Rivals, TSN and Zoom. These are distinguished from portal sites, which cover all sites from one central home page, as the networks have distinct channels dedicated to individual sports. Many of these sites are slick, highly branded and ooze expensive design qualities.

While sports-related fan-sites continue to proliferate and offer alternative views to the mainstream, official Websites for many sports, such as cricket, are increasingly created by one central agency which controls the majority of team and individuals' sites.

Sport still manages to bring the world together, and it can be great fun seeing how the sport of your choice is represented in other countries. In the main we have concentrated on sites of national or international interest. The vast majority of local sports clubs have not been included due to space limitations and because this publication is aimed at an international audience. However, local club details can almost certainly be found via the association, federation or directory sites included for each sport. The few local sites that have been included are present because they provide information of interest to a wider audience.

NETWORKS

There are a host of different sports networks, each with different interconnected channels or zones dedicated to individual sports. Each network channel usually has its own domain and identity within a branded framework, and will sometimes be linked to the other channels in the network. Often, networks are aimed at a particular country audience, focusing coverage on the national team leagues and championships.

www.rivals.net

The European-focused Rivals network is owned by Chrysalis and written by expert fan editors. This network of independent sites covers some of the lesser reported sports, such as Australian Rules Football, cycling and speedway as well as the usual soccer, cricket and rugby.

www.sportal.com
Sportal's model is driven by region, with a flexible approach, depending on the breadth of each sport and the information needs of the fans. Rather than imposing a rigid format on all its sites, Sportal tailors according to need, with eleven own-brand regional sites covering Africa, Asia and Europe in a breadth of languages. Sportal also operates Scrum, the global rugby union site, and has partnerships with specific soccer teams, such as Bayern Munich and Real Madrid. One of the best and most impressive sports networks.🄵

www.sports.com
Football, golf, cricket, rugby union, tennis and F1 coverage.

www.sportsnews.com
Overview site for the sports section of the vast WorldNews.com network. Links to WN sites for a large selection of sports, including sumo, surf and swimming, along with all the other mainstream sports you would expect.

www.teamtalk.com
UK-based network of international channels for football, rugby and horse racing from a large contingent of in-house sports journalists.🄵

PORTALS

Sports portal sites cover many sports from one central Website, aiming to provide an overview, rather than a frag-mented service.

www.110sport.com/sport
Not a huge player in the Web sports scene, 110sport

provides coverage of golf and snooker associated with the sports management and events promotion side of their business. Associated sites include women's golf information at **www.ladieseuropeantour.com**.

www.espn.go.com
MSN's main sports portal.

www.radiosport.com
Excellent links site connected to an exhaustive group of sports radio stations around the globe. Also provides links to newspaper sports coverage.**ⓕ**

www.sportnz.co.nz
New Zealand specific portal.

www.sportserver.com
Covering all the major US sports.

www.sportsline.com
US-oriented general sports coverage.

www.sportspages.com
Collected US sports journalism.

ADVENTURE SPORTS

The majority of the sites here are for non-competitive personal endurance sports, such as mountaineering and trail hiking.

www.bhpa.co.uk
British Hang Gliding and Paragliding Association's site.

www.bungeezone.com
Worldwide listing of bungee jumping opportunities in this amiable amateur site.

www.dropzone.com
Skydiving site.

www.explore.com
Attractive site with many quality features and photos
covering hiking, biking, climbing, skiing, snowboarding,
endurance, water sports and adventure travel. Send good
looking travel postcards by e-mail from this site. **F**

www.mountainzone.com
Covers snowboarding, mountain biking, hiking, skiing and
climbing.

www.pasa.f2s.com
Find out about the world of parachuting in South Africa.

www.thebackpacker.com
Reviews of North American trail hikes, with links to all the
National Parks. Good looking site. **F**

www.thebmc.co.uk
This British Mountaineering Council site is well designed with
lots of information for mountaineers, including club details
and medical advice. **F**

AMERICAN FOOTBALL

www.bcafl.org
The official British Collegiate American Football site.

www.isport.uk.com/amfootball/bsl
Aka Gridironuk.com, the British Senior League's official site
includes match reviews and all the latest news.

www.nfl.com
Arguably, the most important site for American Football –
news, chat and films of the National Football League. **F**

www.superbowl.com
Part of the NFL network. Contains up-to-the-minute news,
with audio and video coverage of Florida's Superbowl
tournament.

ANGLING

www.anglersnet.co.uk
No pun intended at the UK's online fishing magazine. Club directory, fishing reports and lots of information.

www.fisheries.co.uk
Guide to coarse and game fishing in the UK.

www.fishing.co.uk
Claims to be 'Europe's largest internet angling magazine'.

www.fishnet.com.au
More punning with this fishing site from Australia.

www.fishsearch.com
Directory site that aims to bring together the Web's fishing community.

www.the-nfa.org.uk
Home of the UK's National Federation of Anglers.

ARCHERY

archeryaustralia.bizland.com
The national controlling body for Archery Australia.

usa.archery.start4all.com
Straightforward links page to archery organisations in the USA.

www.archery.org
The official Website of the International Archery Federation (FITA – Fédération Internationale de Tir à l'Arc). Includes world record and ranking lists, and a useful international links page.

www.archery-ifaa.com
The International Field Archery Association Website.

www.archerynz.co.nz
Well designed site of Archery New Zealand, which holds national championships for target, field, clout and indoor archery. Includes sections on tournament results, national records and club Web pages.

www.fca.ca
The Federation of Canadian Archers.

www.gnas.org
The official Website of the governing body for the Olympic sport of archery in the UK.

www.nfaa-archery.org
US National Field Archery Association.

www.usarchery.org
The US national governing body for archery, the National Archery Association.

ATHLETICS

www.athletics.org.au
Well laid out site of the governing body for athletics in
Australia which includes chat, audio and video facilities and
photos as well as clubs, schools and indigenous programs.🅕

www.athletics.org.nz
Dull site of Athletics New Zealand, the national body
promoting athletics.

www.athleticscanada.com
Official Website of Athletics Canada.

www.athleticsnet.co.za
Attractively designed South African athletics news and
information site.

www.athleticsnet.com
Guide to UK athletics, including features about athletic
events, athlete profiles and a lively discussion site. Check out
the unexpected Games Zone.🅕

www.athletix.net
Very useful and comprehensive internationally oriented site
from Greece. Includes photos, statistics, and an exhaustive
results archive.🅕

www.commonwealthgames.com
Official site for the Manchester Commonwealth Games 2002.

www.coolrunning.com.au
An original Aussie site created by runners for runners,
including ultra-marathons and mountain running information.

www.gbrathletics.com
Statistics lists for British athletics.

www.iaaf.org
International Association of Athletics Federation's colourful site.

www.london-marathon.co.uk
This innovative London Marathon site includes video and audio clips, and photographs of one of the world's finest urban marathon events.

www.olympics.org.uk
Professional looking British Olympics Association site with all the information you would expect.

www.runnersguide.co.za
A runners' guide to road racing in South Africa.

www.runnersweb.com
A detailed runner and triathlon resource site.

www.runnersworld.co.uk
Website of the UK magazine that provides information and advice for all levels of runner.

www.runtrackdir.com
Directory of over 600 running tracks in the UK. Also includes a UK athletics club Website directory.

www.thesprinter.rivals.net
Athletics channel of the Rivals network.

www.triathletemag.com
Californian-based site which includes tips, training and nutrition advice, as well as triathletics news.

www.triathlon.org
The excellent site of the International Triathlon Union, representing over 100 affiliated national federations around the world. Includes access to clips and live Webcasts. **ⓕ**

www.ukathletics.org
Well designed site of UK Athletics, the national governing body.

AUSTRALIAN RULES FOOTBALL

www.afl.com.au
The official Australian Football League Website, with lots of
audio clips and photos.

www.iafc.org.au
Basic old-fashioned site of the International Australian
Football Confederation, which coordinates and develops the
sport internationally.

www.realfooty.theage.com.au
Australian Rules Football service of The Age, Melbourne's
daily newspaper.

BADMINTON

The world's fastest racquet sport has come a long way since
it was known as shuttlecock and battledore.

www.badminton.ca
The old-style site of Badminton Canada is available in French
and English.

www.badmintoncentral.com
International news and links.

www.badmintonuk.ndo.co.uk
This independently run site includes association and club
directories.

www.badzone.co.uk
Home of the international and UK national badminton clubs
directory.

www.baofe.co.uk
The Badminton Association of England covers news of
national events, rankings, and includes the complete laws of
badminton.

www.intbadfed.org
International Badminton Federation site.

www.usabadminton.org
All you need to know about badminton in the USA.

BASEBALL

baseballhalloffame.org
Website of the baseball national museum at Cooperstown,
New York.

www.baseball-links.com
With over 8,000 baseball links, this site has received over 5
million visitors.

www.baseball-reference.com
Baseball facts and stats aplenty.

www.heckledepot.com
Baseball barbs and heckles duly documented.

www.hotstovediner.com
The place for baseball opinion and heated chat.

www.mlb.com
Official site of Major League Baseball.**❻**

BASKETBALL

world.telebasket.com
Comprehensive site for worldwide basketball information.
Extensive links to international telebasket information sites.**❻**

www.basketballengland.org.uk
News from the official site of England Basketball.

www.bbl.org.uk
The British Basketball League.

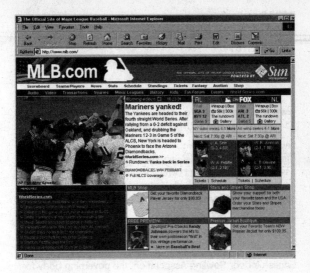

www.britball.com
A broader sweep from this site covering British and Irish basketball and the British Basketball League.

www.nba.com
The site for news and commentary about the US National Basketball Association.

www.nwba.org
US National Wheelchair Basketball Association.

www.wnba.com
Women's National Basketball Association, sister site to nba.com.

BOWLS

bowlingaroundaustralia.com
This travelogue site is also home to the Australian Lawn
Bowls Directory, listing some 2,000 clubs.⑤

bowls.sportingpulse.com/bowlsnz
Information for the New Zealand bowling community.

www.bowlsamerica.org
The official site of the United States Lawn Bowls Association.

www.bowlscanada.com
Site of Bowls Canada Boulingrin, the Canadian sport
association overseeing bowls, including the promotion and
development of lawn bowls, lawn bowling, indoor bowls,
short mat bowls and carpet bowls.

www.bowlsengland.com
Pedestrian site from the English Bowling Association.

www.eiba.co.uk
English Indoor Bowling Association, the governing body for
men's level-green indoor bowls.

BOXING

Along with soccer, boxing is one of the sports at the forefront
of the drive towards greater use of broadband connections as
more live fights are broadcast over the Web.

frankwarren.tv
On-demand video channel featuring archive material,
sponsored by promoter Frank Warren.

www.boxing-monthly.co.uk
The online version of the international boxing magazine
includes over 100 archived articles.

www.boxmag.com
Confusing combination of *Electronic Boxing Weekly*

magazine and sales pitch for computer-based boxing simulation program.

www.britishboxing.com
Readable information about British boxing, including boxer profiles, features, fight reports and archives.

www.cyberboxingzone.com
Amiably idiosyncratic site that includes the Boxing Encyclopaedia and *Wail!* boxing journal.❻

www.heavyweights.co.uk
Online magazine dedicated to top weight division boxers worldwide.

www.houseofboxing.com
This excellent site includes HOBtv, message boards and chat, as well as commentary from respected columnists.

www.iboboxing.com
International Boxing Organisation official Website.

www.wbaonline.com
World Boxing Association official Website.

www.worldboxingfed.com
World Boxing Federation official Website.

CRICKET

www.clickcricket.com
Cricket portal from India.

www.cricket4.com
The UK's Channel 4 television coverage site.

www.cricket.org
Website of CricInfo which has cricket coverage on the Web firmly under its control. It certainly provides the most comprehensive international coverage around, with sites for

eight of the ten Test playing countries. Generating phenomenal traffic, this site is one of the most visited on the Web. CricInfo also provides live audio and video coverage of matches. Check out the site map for a full listing of all the sites under the CricInfo banner, including first-class teams and, amongst others, the cricket Associations of Chile and Israel.🄵

www.cricketer.co.uk
Online version of *The Cricketer International* magazine.

www.cricketworld.com
Useful cricket portal, with the infamous Billy Bhatt.

www.cricketworld.com.au
A similar name for this Australian site, but here the specialisation is in statistics, and computer ratings and analysis.

www.cricnet.com
Official Website of the Professional Cricketers' Association.

www.howstat.com.au
Cricket statistics site from Australia.

www.johnners.com
A celebration of the life of Brian 'Johnners' Johnston, the BBC's voice of cricket until his death in 1994.

www.lanka.net/cricket
Sri Lanka's cricket information site.

www.mcc.org.au
Official site of the Melbourne Cricket Club.

www.thatscricket.com
An Indian emphasis on this site affiliated to **indiainfo.com**.

www.wisden.com
The cricket bible moves from the nineteenth-century into the

twenty-first with this impressive new online site. Plenty of
free information, plus an option to subscribe to the almanac
archives.**G**

Other cricket sites:

www.cricket.com
www.cricketbase.com
www.cricketcrazy.co.uk
www.gentlemansgame.com
www.khel.com
www.thewicket.com

CYCLING

nz.cyclistinfo.com
News for New Zealand cycle enthusiasts.

www.adv-cycling.org
The Adventure Cycling Association's site includes US
National Bicycle Route Network information.

www.bcf.uk.com
Disappointing site from the British Cycling Federation, the
governing body of cycle sport in the UK.

www.bfa.asn.au
Bicycle Federation of Australia.

www.bicyclingmagazine.com
Online version of the best-selling US cycling magazine.

www.bmxaustralia.com.au
Trendy design for this site supported by the Australian Sports
Commission.

www.canadian-cycling.com
Well laid out site from the Canadian Cycling Association.**G**

www.cyclecanada.com
Information about cycling in Canada, including Directory of Cycle Clubs and news of the Tour du Canada.

www.cycling.org.au
Australian Cycling Federation, the governing body for competitive road, track and mountain biking.

www.cyclingnews.com
Extensive cycle racing news and results analysis at this site from Australia.

www.cyclingnz.org.nz
This excellent site from New Zealand includes a useful maps and trails feature, and a sports science section.**❶**

www.cyclo-cross.co.uk
Straightforward Website for cyclo-cross in Britain.

www.ebmx.com
Site for BMX bikers.

www.letour.fr
Le Tour de France official site.

www.mountainbike.co.nz
The New Zealand Mountain Bike Web includes park track maps and magazine links.

www.rttc.org.uk
The UK's Road Time Trials Council.

www.uci.ch
Impressive site from the Union Cycliste Internationale (International Cycling Union), including competition results and rankings.**❶**

DARTS

www.bdodarts.com
British Darts Organisation.

www.cyberdarts.com
This magazine-style site may not look very pretty, but there's a lot of info here, including a tournament archive, the fundamentals of darts, and articles by Dartoid, darts' very own Beat poet.

www.cyberdarts.com/ado
American Darts Organization.

www.dartswdf.com
World Darts Federation site, including world rankings.

www.dartsworld.com
Limited online magazine.

www.dfadarts.cjb.net
Darts Federation of Australia.

www.englanddarts.f9.co.uk
The world of English darts.

www.idpa.net
The site of the International Dart Player Association includes comprehensive links to darts sites worldwide.

www.toetheoche.co.uk
A bit of a rarity this – a well-designed darts site. Sadly, its independence looks set to be lost as it becomes part of EuroSports online and is renamed Darts365.

EQUESTRIAN
General equestrian sites

www.bef.co.uk
The British Equestrian Federation is the recognised governing body of equestrian sport in Britain.

www.cyberhorse.net.au
General directory from Australia for all things horse, including Forums, Form Guide and *Racing Chronicle*.

www.equestrianfederation.com.au
Equestrian Federation of Australia.

www.equiworld.net
This nicely designed site provides general advice on horse care, training and education for horse and rider, explanations of all equestrian sports and an informative e-zine.❺

www.horsenews.com
Aka *The Equestrian Times*. Much of the information in this site is off limits except to paying subscribers.

www.horsesport.ie
Equestrian Federation of Ireland.

www.kickon.com
This imaginatively named site includes an Ask The Experts section offering comprehensive and expert equestrian nutrition and veterinary information, with useful addresses and a free advice service. Also includes news reports and results, message board and chat facilities.❺

www.uset.org
Heavily designed site of the United States Equestrian Team.

OTHER GENERAL EQUESTRIAN SITES:

www.ahsa.org
www.equestria.net
www.equestrian.ca
www.equestrian.co.uk
www.equestrianonline.com
www.eventingnews.com
www.horsetalk.co.nz

Dressage
www.cadora.ca
Canadian Dressage Owners and Riders Association.

www.dressagecanada.org
Attractive site providing information about the development
of dressage in Canada.

www.usdf.org
United States Dressage Foundation.

www.worlddressage.com
Launched by a consortium of volunteer dressage trainers,
riders and enthusiasts based in three countries, the Dressage
World directory provides comprehensive international links
relating to the sport of dressage.🅕

Flat racing

www.ausracing.net.au
This Australian site also covers Europe and the USA.

www.britishracingnews.com
Well-designed site providing heaps of information, including
an explanation of betting terms, plus a regular quiz.🅕

www.horseracing.net
Downmarket ads mar this useful worldwide directory of horse
racing links.

www.irish-racing.com
Coverage of Irish racing, live results and starting prices.

www.racecourse.com
Stored race audio files at the horse racing branch of
radiosport.com.

www.racingpost.co.uk
Clear accessible site from Mirror Group Newspapers.

www.thelatemail.com.au
Australian site providing form information.

www.turfmonthly.com.au
Online version of Australia's popular racing magazine.

OTHER FLAT RACING INFORMATION SITES:

nzgallops.sports-reports.com
www.australianracing.com
www.auzform.com.au
www.flatstats.co.uk
www.racecafe.co.nz
www.race-horses.com
www.racenews.co.uk
www.racetips365.com
www.racewatch.co.nz
www.theracingpages.org.uk

COURSES

Most flat racing courses around the world have their own Websites. Here's a small selection.

www.aintree.co.uk
Aintree is one of thirteen UK courses that can be accessed via this route into the Racecourse Holdings Trust site.

www.ascot-authority.co.uk
Ascots racecourse's regal site.

www.cheltenham.co.uk
Cheltenham racecourse Website, home of UK national hunt racing.

www.comeracing.co.uk
Turn up your speakers for a personal introduction to the informative but idiosyncratically designed site of the Racecourse Association. Contains details of all of Britain's 59 racecourses.

www.curragh.ie
Home to the Irish Derby.

www.goodwood.co.uk
Horse racing is just one of the many sports hosted by Goodwood.

GOVERNING BODIES

home.jockeyclub.com
More than a century old, the US Jockey Club oversees thoroughbred registration.

www.bhb.co.uk
British Horse Racing Board, UK racing's governing body.

www.iha.ie
Irish Horse Racing Authority site, including details of race fixtures and course.

www.jockeyclubsa.co.za
The Jockey Club of Southern Africa site is informative with all the latest news about racing in South Africa, as well as trainer, jockey and horse statistics.

www.thejockeyclub.co.uk
Established in 1752, the Jockey Club is the regulatory authority for horse racing in the UK.

www.turfclub.ie
Irish Turf Club, Ireland's regulatory body for horse racing.

Harness racing

www.harness.org.au
Guide to harness racing in Australia.

www.standardbredcanada.ca
Body established to supervise, record, store and distribute information on all registered Standardbreds and to promote harness racing in Canada.

www.trotworld.com
A comprehensive Web directory of harness racing. **❻**

www.ustrotting.com
Popular site of the US Trotting Association.

Show jumping

www.bsja.co.uk
Website of the British Showjumping Association.

www.hickstead.co.uk
Website of one of the world's most important showjumping venues.

www.hoys.co.uk
Website of the Horse of the Year show, the event established in 1949 which hosts the finals of the UK's most prestigious showjumping championships.

www.nhs.org
Founded in 1883, the National Horse Show is the USA's oldest indoor horse show.

www.showjump.com
News and information about international showjumping from this US site, including a dynamic database of US and international grand prix.

www.tournamentofchampions.ca
Canada's major showjumping event.

FENCING

No longer one of the glory sports, fencing nevertheless has a long and esteemed history and flourishing club-level activities.

members.aol.com/ComFence
A few useful links on this small site from the Commonwealth Fencing Federation.

www.baf-fencing.com
Coaching organisation for fencing in the UK.

www.fencing.net/pages/clubs/swordsclub
Over 700 international fencing links.

www.fencingonline.com
Modern information site, outlining the basics of the sport and
an online store for all those fencing accoutrements.**Ⓕ**

www.fencinguk.net
Resource site for UK fencers, including e-mail group.

www.fie.ch
Popular French-language official site from the Federation
Internationale d'Escrime, aka the International Fencing
Federation.

www.kmoser.com/cflist.htm
An alternative to modern fencing, this mailing list is for
classical fencing and traditional swordsmanship aficionados,
with particular reference to French, Italian and Spanish
schools of the 15th–19th centuries.

National fencing sites

www.fencing.ca	Canada
www.fencing.org.nz	New Zealand
www.britishfencing.com	United Kingdom
www.usfencing.org	United States

FIELD HOCKEY

www.fieldhockey.com
Excellent worldwide hockey coverage.**Ⓕ**

www.fieldhockeytournament.com
This US site aspires to unite hockey players from around the
world via a young players' tournament.

www.hockeyonline.co.uk
The English Hockey Association's simple but well designed
site provides 'Hockeyville', a comprehensive list of English
Hockey Clubs, with 'café-bar' discussion forums.

www.hockeyweb.co.uk
Inclusive site that welcomes anyone with an interest in hockey.

GOLF
General golf sites
nzopen.nzoom.com
Information about and coverage of the New Zealand Open.

www.englishgolfunion.org
Established in 1924, the EGU is the governing body for male amateur golf in England. It arranges major amateur tournaments and looks after the interests of over 1,890 affiliated golf clubs and some 730,000 club members.

www.golf-foundation.org
Charity originating from 1951 committed to making golf accessible to young people throughout the British Isles.

www.golfonline.com
Informative online US mag from the editors of *Golf* magazine.

www.golftoday.co.uk
Europe's online golf magazine, part of the golftoday network of golf sites.

www.golfzone.co.uk
From Myzi sports consultancy, this link site claims to connect with some 30,000 European Websites associated with golf.

www.gui.ie
The Golfing Union of Ireland.

www.lpga.com
Official Website of the Ladies Professional Golf Association, the longest running women's sports association in the world.

www.opengolf.com
Official Website of the Open Championship at Royal Lytham & St Anne's.

www.pga.com
Official site of the PGA of America.

www.scottishgolf.com
Everything you could need to know about golf in Scotland, including tips, columnists, courses and a history of golf. Links to the Scottish Golf Union and the Scottish Ladies Golfing Association Websites.

www.thegolfchannel.com
Website of the Florida-based cable and satellite channel, which features the ever-present personalisable Visitor's Locker which includes a news ticker, multi-tour leader boards and current weather forecasts.

www.usga.org
Formed in 1894, the United States Golf Association is a non-profit making organisation run by golfers for golfers. This is the organisation that, along with the Royal and Ancient Golf Club of St Andrews, Scotland, writes and interprets the rules of golf.

OTHER GENERAL GOLF SITES:
www.ausgolf.com.au
www.golfing.co.nz
www.worldgolf.com

Professional golfers
These official sites are not afraid to be commercial enterprises and are usually selling consultancy, merchandise, golf course design services or something similar. There are some interesting but limited authorised biographical details and images to keep the fans happy.

www.garyplayer.com
www.nicklaus.com
www.phil-mickelson.com
www.seveballesteros.com

www.shark.com
www.tigerwoods.com

GYMNASTICS

www.american-gymnast.com
New journal written from the insider's point of view and with a personal touch.**F**

www.baga.co.uk
Formed as long ago as 1888, the British Amateur Gymnastics Association, the recognised governing body for the sport in the UK, is now known as British Gymnastics. There is also another site at **www.isport.uk.com/gymnastics/bg.**

www.fig-gymnastics.com
Lots of useful information about the various gymnastic disciplines at the multi-language International Gymnastics Federation Website.

www.girlsgymnastics.com
Colour, kitsch and dancing stars at this entertaining advert for a gymnastics summer camp in Texas.

www.gymmedia.com
European gymnastics are comprehensively covered at this busy site.

www.gymnastics.org.au
Australian Gymnastics Federation.

www.gymnastics-ueg.org
European Union of Gymnastics.

www.gym-routines.com
Unusual site providing gym routines from around the world.

www.ighof.com
International Gymnastics Hall of Fame.

www.intlgymnast.com
Online version of the USA's *International Gymnast* magazine.

www.tramp-net.com
This community-run Website contributed to by around a hundred people worldwide has become influential in the world of trampolining.

www.usa-gymnastics.org
National body for gymnastics in the USA.

Other gymnastics sites
www.geocities.com/ausgymfan
www.gym-links.com
www.gymn.ca
www.gymn-forum.com
www.gymnstands.net

ICE HOCKEY

www.azhockey.com
Comprehensive facts, figures and links in this UK-based compendium.

www.canadianhockey.ca
The Canadian Ice Hockey Association is the national governing body for amateur hockey.

www.hockeydb.com
This excellent site is a huge repository of US hockey data, including stats and player lists, plus a fascinating trading card archive and unique team logo database, and a new player awards and trophies archive. **F**

www.icehockeyuk.co.uk
Ice Hockey UK was formed to take over from the British Ice Hockey Association as the National Governing Body and is affiliated to the International Ice Hockey Federation. This well

designed site includes interviews with Ice Hockey personalities by Miss Conduct.

www.iceweb.co.uk
The British Ice Hockey Superleague was established in 1996, since when the sport has grown exponentially in the UK. This Website includes a beginners' guide and rules.**F**

www.iihf.com
Founded in 1908, the International Ice Hockey Federation includes the associations which govern the sport. Included here is a history of the sport and details of IIHF tournaments.

www.inthecrease.com
US ice hockey news and features.

www.nhl.com
Impressive US National Hockey League site with links to

each of 30 individual NHL team sites, plus broadband and
radio broadcasts.**❻**

www.puck-off.com
How can you resist with a name like this? This independent
UK site highlights the entertainment aspects of ice hockey
with its 'View from the Bar' column and 'Roger's Bits'.

Other ice hockey sites
www.britnatleague.co.uk
www.usahockey.com

ICE SKATING
figure-skating.com
California-based magazine-style skating portal with links to a
network of associated skating sites, including a forum and
chat about skating, and SkateRadio.**❻**

www.bladesonice.com
Online version of North American ice skating magazine.

www.cfsa.ca
Skate Canada, the largest figure skating body in the world,
provides national team and results data.

www.frogsonice.com/skateweb
Independent link site featuring articles, news and a
worldwide rinks and clubs index.

www.ice.co.za
Personal page constructed around synchronised ice skating
in South Africa.

www.iceskating.org.uk
UK National Ice Skating Association.

www.ifsmagazine.com
Website of the US magazine *International Figure Skating*.

www.isa.org.au
Ice Skating Australia.

www.iskater.com
Skating search engine, video, games, quizzes, comics and the FS World message board can be found at this useful site from Canada. **F**

www.isu.org
Swiss-based International Skating Union.

www.skatingincanada.com
Information and news about Canadian Figure Skating.

www.usfsa.org
The official Web home of the US Figure Skating Association includes biographies of the US team.

www.worldskatingmuseum.org
The World Figure Skating Museum and Hall of Fame, based in Colorado.

Speed skating

www.speedskating.ca
'Patinage de Vitesse', otherwise known as speed skating, can be traced back over a thousand years, according to the history section of this site from Canada.

www.usspeedskating.org
The Olympic sport of speed skating in the US.

Other ice skating sites

www.geocities.com/theskateblade
www.iceskatingintnl.com

MARTIAL ARTS

For the uninitiated, the self-defence sports of the Martial Arts can prove somewhat confusing in all their various incarnations. The following sites should provide a general overview of the many different aspects of the sport.

General martial arts

www.bccma.org.uk
The site of the British Council for Chinese Martial Arts includes a UK national schools directory.

www.blackbeltmag.com
Online version of US martial arts magazine.

www.budoseek.net
Martial Arts directory site with links to discussion groups, publications, supplies and services.

www.maaust.com
Martial Arts in Australia, including discussion forum, directory and events calendar.

www.mararts.org
United States Martial Arts Association.

www.martialarts-guide.com
History and philosophies from Aikido to Viet Vo Dao.

www.martialinfo.com
Highly energetic site packed full of information. ★

www.mawn.net
The Martial Arts Worldwide Network.

www.usadojo.com
This site attempts to unravel the mysteries of the various national versions of martial arts, including those from Brazil, Indonesia and Russia, as well as the more expected places.

www.usmaf.org
United States Martial Arts Foundation which provides discussion forums and links.

Aikido

www.aikido-baa.org.uk
British Aikido Association.

www.aikidofaq.com
US directory of Aikido information and resources.

www.aikikai.org
The Aikido world headquarters in Japan.

www.aikiweb.com
News and links for the Aikido Internet community.❶

www.nataikidofed.org.uk
UK national Aikido Federation.

Judo

www.britishjudo.org.uk
www.judocanada.org
www.judoinfo.com
www.worldjudo.org

MOTOR SPORTS

General motor sports

www.autoracing1.com
CART, NASCAR and F1 news.

www.autosport.com
Online version of the popular UK magazine.

www.linksheaven.com
Huge collection of Formula 1, CART and NASCAR links.❶

www.motorsport.co.za
The controlling body of motor sport in South Africa.

www.motorsport.com
US-based site with heaps of international information.❶

www.ten-tenths.com
Impressive volunteer-run British site providing a links directory, circuit guide and discussion forum, plus a multimedia and cartoon archive.**ⓕ**

www.ukmotorsport.com
Lots of UK motor sports links.

www.worldmotorsport.com
Discussion forum and directory.

Bikes
www.amasuperbike.com
www.british-superbikes.co.uk
www.cyclenews.com

Formula 1

GENERAL F1 NEWS AND INFORMATION SITES
A huge number of high quality, well designed sites, both professional and amateur, official and unofficial, exist to provide the Formula 1 enthusiast with enough information to OD many times over. Most are updated with exemplary speed on race day. The short and instantly recognisable phrase, 'F1', helps locate the Formula 1 sites and is ubiquitous in the URLs.

www.alphaf1.com
www.atlasf1.com
www.dailyf1.com
www.f1.on.net
www.f1express.com
www.f1fanclub.co.uk
www.f1i.com
www.f1-live.com
www.f1-news.com
www.f1nutter.com
www.f1racing.net

www.f1-racing.org
www.f1-world.co.uk
www.fia.com
www.formula1.com
www.itv-f1.com
www.planet-f1.com
www.totalf1.com
www.webf1.net
www.zoomf1.com

FORMULA 1 TEAMS

www.arrows.com
www.benettonf1.com
www.britishamericanracing.com
www.jordangp.com
www.ferrariworld.com/cgi-bin/fworld.dll/ferrariworld/scripts/
racing/ferrari_team.jsp
www.jaguar-racing.com
www.mclaren.com
www.minardi.it
www.prostgp.com
www.sauber.ch
www.williamsf1.co.uk

DRIVERS

www.a-senna.com
www.davidcoulthard.com
www.eddieirvine365.com
www.hakkinen.net
www.jarnotrulli.com
www.johnnyherbert.co.uk
www.jpmontoya.com
www.jv-world.com
www.mikasalo.net
www.pedrodiniz.com
www.racecar.co.uk/jensonbutton

www.schumacher-fanclub.com
www.verstappen.nl
www.wurz.com

OTHER FORMULA 1 SITES

www.brit-f1.co.uk
www.ddavid.com/formula1
www.fia.com
www.fosa.org

Indy racing

www.indyracingleague.com

NASCAR

www.nascar.com

Rally

www.britishrally.co.uk
www.motorsport.co.uk
www.rally-live.com
www.rallyzone.com
www.worldrally.net

NETBALL

netballnz.co.nz
www.england-netball.co.uk
www.indoornetball.org.au
www.isport.ca/netball/cana
www.netball.asn.au
www.netball.org
www.netballscotland.freeserve.co.uk
www.netball.tv
www.netballuk.co.uk
www.usanetball.com
www.welshnetball.org.uk

RUGBY

Rugby League

WORLD RUGBY LEAGUE

www.playtheball.com
Sportal's Rugby League channel.

www.rleague.com
Launched in 1997, this is probably the best rugby league world portal site. **ⓕ**

www.rugbyleaguer.co.uk
Online version of the popular UK magazine.

NATIONAL SITES

www.nz.rleague.com
Comprehensive coverage for New Zealand.

www.bulldogs.com.au
New South Wales club site.

www.bronconet.com
'Totally unofficial' Website of Australia's Brisbane Broncos.

www.hullkr.co.uk
Web home of the UK's Hull Kingston Rovers.

www.nrl.com.au
Australia's official National Rugby League site.

www.nzleague.co.nz
Unofficial site for the New Zealand league.

www.rleague.com/southafrica
South Africa's rugby league site, hosted by Rleague.com.

www.rugbyleague.co.nz
Coverage of Rugby League for Australia and New Zealand.

www.rugby-league.org
UK's rugby football league.

Rugby Union

WORLD RUGBY UNION
www.itv-rugby.co.uk
International coverage from UK television's rugby-covering channel.

www.planet-rugby.com
Comprehensive international portal that supplies content to other sites, including ITV-rugby.❻

www.rugbyheaven.com
Portal from Australia.

www.rugbyworld.com
Online version of the best-selling magazine.

www.scrum.com
From the Sportal network.

NATIONAL SITES

www.rugby.com.au	Australia
www.rugbycanada.ca	Canada
www.ffr.fr	France
www.irfu.ie	Ireland
www.rugbynews.co.nz	New Zealand
www.sarugby.net	South Africa
www.rfu.com	United Kingdom
www.usarugby.org	United States
www.irb.org	International

SNOOKER, POOL AND BILLIARDS

www.bca-pool.com
Billiard Congress of America.

www.snookernet.com
The best independent site for snooker, with news, results, reviews and a potted history of the sport.❻

www.wpbsa.com
World Snooker is the governing body for professional snooker worldwide.

Other
www.110sport.com/snooker
www.billsnook.com.au
www.embassysnooker.com

SOCCER

Football or soccer? There are a huge number of sites dedicated to the world's number one sport, whatever you call it.

World soccer portals
soccerbullet.com
www.dailysoccer.com
www.dottwo.com/onetouch
www.soccernet.com
www.soccer-sites.com
www.soccerstats.com
www.womensoccer.com
www.worldsoccernews.com
www.zoomsoccer.com

OTHER WORLD SITES
www.fifa.com
www.uefa.com
www.worldcuparchive.com

National sites

UNITED KINGDOM

United Kingdom portals

football.guardian.co.uk
www.fa-premier.com
www.football365.com
www.footballnews.co.uk
www.footymad.net
www.fromtheterrace.co.uk
www.scotprem.com
www.soccerbase.com
www.soccerupdate.com
www.weeballs.com
www.wsc.co.uk
www.zoofootball.com

United Kingdom clubs

You can observe the countdown to the anticipated fuller broadband connection that doesn't seem to have really happened yet in the UK, with both Chelsea and Liverpool providing WebTV coverage.

www.chelseafc.co.uk
www.evertonfc.com
www.hibs.co.uk
www.lcfc.co.uk
www.liverpoolfc.tv
www.lufc.com
www.manutd.com
www.nufc.co.uk

Other United Kingdom sites

www.football-league.co.uk
www.fsa.org.uk
www.the-fa.org

UNITED STATES AND CANADA PORTALS

www.canadakicks.com
www.mlsnet.com
www.soccer365.com
www.socceramerica.com

Football personalities

Finally, a very small selection of Websites about those who have influenced the world of football, or soccer.

www.brianclough.com
www.ginola14.com
www.icons.com
www.royoftherovers.com

SQUASH

Squash portals

squash.start4all.com
Links to clubs in many different countries.

www.eyesquash.com
The Eye Group holds the rights to many of the world's top squash events.

www.guide-to-squash.org
Information and tips on playing squash.

www.squashchampions.com
Site saluting the sport's stars of today and yesterday.

www.squashlinks.co.uk
International squash links.

www.squashnow.com
News, reports, results and commentary.

www.squashplayer.co.uk
An international perspective from the online version of this UK-based magazine.

www.squashtalk.com
Global source of independent squash news and information.

www.supersquash.com
Lots of worldwide links at this directory site.

www.wispa.net
Women's International Squash Players Association.

www.worldsquash.org
Official site of the World Squash Federation.

National sites

www.irishsquash.com
www.squash.ca
www.squash.org.au
www.squashnz.co.nz
www.squashsa.com
www.squashwales.co.uk
www.us-squash.org

SUMO

www.sumoweb.com
Links and insights into the world of sumo.

www.sumoworld.com
Online version of the Japanese sumo magazine.

TABLE TENNIS

www.ctta.ca
Canadian Table Tennis Association.

www.etta.co.uk
English Table Tennis Association.

www.ettu.org
European Table Tennis Union.

www.ittf.com
International Table Tennis Federation.

www.table-tennis.com
Table Tennis directory and search engine.

www.tabletennis.gr
Useful world information about table tennis from this
independently produced site from Greece.**G**

www.tabletennis.org.nz
Table Tennis New Zealand is an integrated body of players,
coaches and administrators.

www.worldtabletennis.com
International Table Tennis news and articles from the World
News network.**G**

www.usatt.org
The US Table Tennis site includes a potted history of the
sport, as well as an online magazine.

TENNIS

www.atptennis.com
Tournament calendars, news and reports from the
Association of Tennis Professionals, the governing body of
the men's professional circuit.**G**

www.crosscourt.com.au
News and a photographic gallery at this site from Australia.

www.itftennis.com
Facts and figures, and rules and regulations from the
London-based International Tennis Federation, the worldwide
governing body of tennis with nearly 200 national associations.

www.lta.org.uk/lta.htm
The Lawn Tennis Association is the governing body of the
sport in Britain.

www.tennis.net
News, gossip, results and column at this Tennis portal.

www.tennisnet.co.za
South African-based tennis news site, hosted by MWeb.

www.tennisnews.com
Results, news and classifieds from US-based Tennis News.

Other tennis sites
www.daviscup.org
www.tennis.com
www.usopen.org
www.wimbledon.com

TENPIN BOWLING

ozbowl.com
Links to information about venues, forums, events and
leagues at Australia's tenpin bowling directory.

www.bowling.org.uk
News, leagues, books and links to British tenpin bowling
sites.

www.bowlingdigital.com
International tenpin bowling facts, figures and records.🄵

www.bowlsearch.com
Bowling search engine and directory.

www.btba.org.uk
British Tenpin Bowling Association.

www.fiq.org
Fédération Internationale des Quilleurs, also known as the
International Bowling Federation, is the world governing body
for ninepin and tenpin bowling.

www.kolumbus.fi/bowwwling
Perhaps the ultimate bowling directory, including links to a
selection of instruction and information sites, as well as news
and tournament and results sites.**❺**

www.stba.org.uk
Scottish Tenpin Bowling Association.

www.tenpin.org
Canadian Bowling Index, including the Canadian Tenpin
Federation's Webpages.

Other tenpin bowling sites
www.bowlingmuseum.com
www.bowlingzone.com
www.bowluk.co.uk

VOLLEYBALL

www.avptour.com
Association of Volleyball Professionals.

www.canoe.ca/SlamVolleyball
Canadian Volleyball news.

www.fivb.ch
International Volleyball Federation.

www.isport.com.au/volleyball/avf
Australian Volleyball Federation.

www.volleyball.ca
Attractive site from Volleyball Canada.**❺**

www.volleyball.org
The layout may be old-fashioned, but this site is packed with
useful information and links.**❺**

www.volleyballmag.com
Online version of the popular magazine.

www.volleyhall.org
According to the Volleyball hall of fame, the sport is over a hundred years old and was originally known as Mintonette.

Other volleyball sites
www.beachmania.com
www.usavolleyball.org
www.vball.net
www.volleyball.com
www.volleyballseek.com

WATER SPORTS

Canoeing
www.bcu.org.uk
British Canoe Union.

www.canoeicf.com
International Canoe Federation.

www.canoekayak.ca
Canadian Canoe Association.

www.usacanoekayak.org
Official site of USACK, the national governing body for canoe and kayak racing in the US.

www.welsh-canoeing.org.uk
In Welsh and English, this well designed site from Canolfan Tryweryn, the National Whitewater Centre, also hosts the Welsh Canoeing Association's Webpages. **F**

OTHER CANOEING SITES
www.canoe.org.au
www.canoefocus.demon.co.uk
www.irishcanoeunion.com
www.kayaksport.co.uk

www.paddlermagazine.com
www.wavelengthmagazine.com

Diving

SPRINGBOARD AND PLATFORM DIVING

www.coolrunning.co.nz/diving
www.diving.asn.au
www.diving.ca
www.usadiving.com
www.usdiving.org

SCUBA AND SUB-AQUA DIVING

www.bsac.com
www.dive-links.co.uk
www.divenet.com
www.divenewzealand.com
www.diverlink.com
www.divermag.com
www.divernet.com
www.divinginaustralia.com.au
www.divinginusa.com
www.madforscuba.com
www.nzscuba.com
www.scubadiving.com
www.scubaduba.com
www.scubaspots.com
www.skin-diver.com
www.subaqua.co.uk
www.undercurrent.org

Rowing

www.ara-rowing.org
UK Amateur Rowing Association.

www.aviron.org
The USA's National Rowing Foundation.

www.hrr.co.uk
This site doesn't really do justice to one of the UK's premier rowing occasions, the Henley Royal Regatta, held annually since 1839.

www.rowersworld.com
Access 50,000 rowing photographs at this rowing portal site from the US.

www.rowingnz.org.nz
This well designed official New Zealand Rowing Association Website provides links to Club listings and is part of the rowing Webring. **F**

www.rrm.co.uk
The Website of Henley's River and Rowing Museum.

www.scottish-rowing.org.uk
The Scottish Amateur Rowing Association.

OTHER ROWING SITES
www.coxless4.com
www.irishrowing.com
www.regatta.rowing.org.uk
www.rowingaustralia.com.au
www.rowinglinks.com
www.rowuk.cjb.net
www.total.rowing.org.uk
www.usrowing.org
www.worldrowers.com

Sailing
www.cyca.com.au
The Cruising Yacht Club of Australia.

www.ista.co.uk
International Sail Training Association, organiser of the Cutty Sark Tall Ships' Races.

www.madforsailing.com
Useful sailing portal site from the UK.🄵

www.rin.org.uk
Royal Institute of Navigation.

www.rya.org.uk
Royal Yachting Association.🄵

www.seahorse.co.uk
Sailing magazine from the UK.

www.ssanz.co.nz
Short Handed Sailing Association of New Zealand.

www.thewya.freeserve.co.uk
The Welsh Yachting Association.

www.uksail.com
UK directory of sailing links.

www.uk-sail.org.uk
UK Sailing Academy.

www.ussailing.org
National governing body of sailing in the US.

www.yacht.co.uk
Yachting link site from UK.

www.yachting.org.au
Australian Yachting Federation.

www.yachtingnz.org.nz
New Zealand's national body for recreational and competitive boating and yachting.

www.ybw.co.uk
Yachting and Boating World.

OTHER SAILING SITES

sailingsource.com
www.apparent-wind.com
www.bwsailing.com
www.catsailor.com
www.cruiser.co.za
www.cruisingworld.com
www.gosailing.co.uk
www.sailing.org
www.sailinglinks.com
www.sailnet.com
www.searoom.com
www.teamracing.org
www.ukdinghyracing.com

Surfing

GENERAL SURF SITES

www.magicsurfbus.com
Turn down your volume for this surf portal.

www.maxpages.com/worldsurfcams
Surf cams links from around the world. This site also has
many other surfing links.

www.surfrider.org
The Surfrider Foundation is a non-profit organisation
dedicated to the protection of beaches, oceans and waves.

www.surftv.com
Surf link site.

www.swell.com
Raft of surf-related information, including cameras,
conditions and weather maps at Surfline. **ⓕ**

www.worldsurfers.com
Online videos and a history of surfing at this international site.

NATIONAL SURF SITES

Australia
www.coastalwatch.com
www.surfcam.com.au
www.surfingaustralia.com
www.surfinglife.net
www.surfingworld.com
www.surfworld.org.au

New Zealand
www.surf.co.nz
www.surfguide.co.nz
www.surfnz.com
www.winzurf.co.nz

United Kingdom
www.a1surf.com
www.bpsauktour.com
www.britsurf.co.uk
www.coldwatersoul.co.uk
www.surfchat.co.uk
www.surfstation.co.uk
www.surf-uk.org.uk

United States
www.surfinfo.com
www.surfingmuseum.org
www.surflink.com

Swimming
www.swiminfo.com
www.swimming.ca
www.swimming.org.au
www.swimnews.com

www.usasynchro.org
www.usswim.org
www.webswim.com
www.worldwideswimming.com

Waterskiing

usawaterski.org
www.aquaskier.com
www.britishwaterski.co.uk
www.iwsf.com
www.planetwaterski.com
www.waterski.ca
www.waterski.com
www.waterski-az.co.uk
www.waterski-uk.com

Windsurfing

watersports-extreme.com
Guide to surfing, canoeing and windsurfing.

www.box.net.au/~jrohde/windsurf
Australian Windsurfing.

www.windsurf.ca
Canadian Master Windsurfers Association and Windsurf
Canada.

www.world-windsurfing.com
Professional Windsurfers Association.

OTHER WINDSURFING SITES

www.americanwindsurfer.com
www.iwindsurf.com
www.windplanet.com
www.windsurfer.com
www.worldwindsurf.com

WINTER SPORTS

Bobsleigh and luge

british-bobsleigh.com
British Bobsleigh Association.

www.bobsledder.com
History of bobsleigh and athlete profiles.

www.bobsleigh.ca
Bobsleigh Canada.

www.bobsleigh.com
International Bobsleigh and Tobogganing Federation.

www.fil-luge.org
International Luge Federation.

www.luge.ca
Luge Canada.

www.usabobsledandskeleton.org
The US Bobsled and Skeleton Federation.

www.usaluge.org
The United States Luge Association.

Skiing and snowboarding

CROSS-COUNTRY SKIING
www.backcountrymagazine.com
www.crosscountryskier.com
www.cross-country-skiing.com
www.hoppet.com.au/xc

SKIING
General skiing sites
best-skiing.co.uk
Ski and snowboarding resorts and holiday fact files.

www.firsttracksonline.com
This ski magazine has been online since 1994.

www.fis-ski.com
International Ski Federation.

www.freeskier.com
Skiing lifestyle mag.

www.hyperski.com
Online skiing and snowboarding magazine.

www.natives.co.uk
Portal for ski seasons resort workers.

www.pistoff.com
Snow, resort and weather reports.

www.skiclub.co.uk
Approaching one hundred years old, the Ski Club of Great Britain provides holiday offers and skiing information and guidance to its members.

www.skimaps.com
Worldwide resort information and online trail maps, together with features, forums and video.**ᶠ**

www.skinet.com
Gear, snow reports, resorts and travel information.

www.skiracing.com
The well designed Ski Racing magazine online site provides international skiing and snowboard race results.**ᶠ**

National Sites

Australia
www.ski.com.au
www.skiingaustralia.org.au

Canada
www.canski.org
www.skicanada.org
www.skicanadamag.com**F**
www.skilinkcanada.com

New Zealand
www.skifreestyle.co.nz
www.ski.net.nz
www.skiracing.org.nz
www.snow.co.nz
www.snowreports.co.nz

United Kingdom
www.ski.co.uk

United States
www.usskiteam.com

SNOWBOARDING

www.boarderzone.co.nz
www.boardtheworld.com
www.feelthepow.com
www.twsnow.com

WRESTLING

Dare we call it a sport?

www.wcw.com
www.wrestlingdotcom.com
www.wwf.com

Transport

The immediacy of the Internet means that it is ideally placed to provide up-to-the minute transport news, including local road reports from WebCams placed to observe the traffic flow, and inbound flight information from airport sites. Rail and coach timetables are now readily available over the Web, as are online booking facilities for most types of public transport, including rail, air and ferry services. Economy airline online direct booking resources are one of the great e-commerce success stories, with savings and discounts being available for bookings made over the Internet.

GENERAL WORLDWIDE TRANSPORT

www.routesinternational.com
Worldwide land, sea and air transport links.

SUBWAYS INTERNATIONAL

These two sites provide links to subway and underground maps worldwide.

www.metropla.net
www.reed.edu/~reyn/transport.html

NATIONAL TRANSPORT
Australia
AIR

www.airportsaustralia.com.au

BUS AND COACH

www.mccaffertys.com.au
www.pixeltech.com.au/firefly

Rail
General Rail
people.enternet.com.au/~cbrnbill/maps/austrail.htm
Detailed passenger rail maps and timetables across
Australia.

www.railpage.org.au/pass.html
Railpass details and links to agents' sites.

Rail Companies
www.cityrail.nsw.gov.au
www.countrylink.nsw.gov.au
www.gsr.com.au
www.staterail.nsw.gov.au
www.traveltrain.qr.com.au

Canada
AIR
www.airportscanada.com

RAIL
General rail
www.railscanada.com
Link page to railway-connected subjects, from rail art and
memorabilia to rail photos.

Rail companies
www.viarail.ca

New Zealand
AIR
www.airportsnewzealand.com

RAIL
www.tranzrailtravel.co.nz
www.travelpass.co.nz

United Kingdom
PUBLIC TRANSPORT GENERAL

www.pti.org.uk
Public Transport Information, providing local and national links to bus, ferry and rail companies and airlines.

AIR
Airports

www.a2bairports.com
Guide to all main UK airports.

www.baa.co.uk
Guide and links to all UK airports administered by BAA.

Budget airlines

www.buzzaway.com
www.easyjet.com
www.go-fly.com
www.ryanair.com

BUS AND COACH

www.gobycoach.com
National Express and Eurolines information.

FERRY

www.brittany-ferries.com
www.dfdsseaways.co.uk
www.ferrybooker.com
www.ferryinformationservice.co.uk
www.ferrysavers.com
www.irishferries.com
www.ponsf.com
www.posl.com
www.seafrance.co.uk
www.stenaline.co.uk

RAIL

General rail

traininformation.co.uk
Links to train information sites.

www.brb.gov.uk
British Railways Board.

www.britrail.com
Details of rail passes for non-UK British rail passengers.

www.chester-le-track.co.uk
Aka nationalrail.com, a curious site from the Chester-le-Street rail station in County Durham, northern England, which provides national network information.

www.delayed.net
An independent online complaints desk campaigning for better UK rail services.

www.nationalrail.co.uk
'26 companies, one network' is the rallying cry of this attempt to provide an official one-stop point for UK rail information, billed as 'the gateway to Britain's National Rail network'.**❻**

www.rail.co.uk
Links to timetables, all train operating companies and rail-associated businesses.

www.railcard.co.uk
UK national railcard information, including Young Persons, Senior, Family, Network and Disabled Persons.

www.railchoice.co.uk
Agent for rail travel tickets and passes for UK passengers travelling in Europe.

www.rail-reg.gov.uk
Office of the Rail Regulator, the independent government

department responsible for the regulation of the railways in the UK.

www.railtrack.co.uk
Railtrack's corporate site includes timetable information.

www.railwaysafety.org.uk
Not-for-profit, wholly-owned subsidiary of Railtrack Group plc.

www.sra.gov.uk
The Strategic Rail Authority, another government department, created in 2001 with a mandate to 'promote and develop the rail network and encourage integration'.

www.thetrainline.com
Gives general rail and timetable information and allows you to book tickets and reserve seats. **ⓕ**

www.totaljourney.com
Plan your journey, book your tickets, and get station information as well as shopping and city guides with this site from FirstGroup.

Rail companies
www.angliarailways.co.uk
www.c2c-online.co.uk
www.centraltrains.co.uk
www.chilternrailways.co.uk
www.connex.co.uk
www.eurostar.co.uk
www.firstnorthwestern.co.uk

www.gner.co.uk
Great North Eastern Railways.

www.great-western-trains.co.uk
First Great Western.

www.midlandmainline.com

www.nirailways.co.uk
Northern Ireland Railways.

www.northern-spirit.co.uk
Arriva Trains Northern.

www.scotrail.co.uk
www.silverlink-trains.com
www.swtrains.co.uk
www.thameslink.co.uk
www.thamestrains.co.uk
www.virgintrains.co.uk
www.wagn.co.uk
www.walesandwest.co.uk

www.yourtrain.co.uk
First Great Eastern.

LONDON
London transport general
www.bbc.co.uk/london/travel
Latest travel news in London from the BBC, including traffic
condition reports from 160 strategically sited jam cams.

www.dlr.co.uk
Docklands Light Railway.

www.londoncyclenetwork.org
Maps, videos and general information about the London
Cycle Network.

www.londontransport.co.uk
The body responsible for delivering an integrated transport
strategy for London.

Underground
www.goingunderground.co.uk

www.thetube.com
www.tubeplanner.com

USA

AIR
www.airportsamerica.com

BUS AND COACH
www.greyhound.com

RAIL

General rail
www.trainweb.com
Popular link site with connections to rail discussion forums,
live railcams and railroad industry sites.

www.usa-by-rail.com
Guide to travelling by Amtrak and VIA trains in US and
Canada.

Rail companies
www.amtrak.com

Road
1010wins.com/trafficcams
Jam cams from New York's news-only channel.

Subways and underground
www.nycsubway.org

Europe
BUS AND COACH
www.busabout.com
www.busweb.com

RAIL
www.eurail.com
www.freedomrail.co.uk
www.raileurope.co.uk
www.seat61.com
www.theglobalrailway.com

Travel

Travel information from around the world can be accessed over the Net, whether it's locating and booking accommodation, or finding out travel-related facts for individual destinations from travel search engines or online guide books. There are also a huge array of online maps to make travel preparation simpler.

ACCOMMODATION
Budget and hostels

www.backpack.co.nz
Backbacker budget hostels in New Zealand.

www.backpackers.ca
Hostels in Canada.

www.backpackers.co.uk
Guide to budget accommodation and backpacker hostels in the UK and Ireland.

www.celtic-accommodation.ie
Budget accommodation booking throughout Ireland and worldwide.

www.cheapaccommodation.com
Limited destinations available.

www.cheapnights.com
Search engine in contact with a number of booking agents.

www.eurocheapo.com
This well designed inexpensive European hotel accommodation site covers only a limited number of cities at the moment, but does it well and in-depth.❶

www.europeanhostels.com
European hostel information.

www.hostelaustralia.com
Budget nights in Australia.

www.hostelhandbook.com
Hostels in the US and Canada.

www.hostels.com
Independent hostel guide and booking service.**F**

www.hostelseurope.com
Guide to independent hostels in Europe.

www.hostelworld.com
Worldwide inexpensive accommodation booking service.**F**

www.laterooms.com
Discount prices on last minute bookings.

www.room-service.co.uk
Cheap hotels in major cities.

www.vip.co.nz
Backpacker accommodation throughout New Zealand.

International

HOSTELLING INTERNATIONAL SITES
www.hostelbooking.com
Booking Network for the International Youth Hostel
Federation.

www.iyhf.org
International Youth Hostelling Federation's site with
information and tips about hostelling worldwide.

NATIONAL
www.hiayh.org
Hostelling International's American Youth Hostels.

www.hihostels.ca
Canada's Hostelling International site.

www.hini.org.uk
Hostelling International Northern Ireland.

www.hisa.org.za
Hostelling International South Africa.

www.irelandyha.org
An Oige, the Youth Hostel Association of Ireland.

www.syha.org.uk
Scottish Youth Hostel Association.

www.yha.com.au
Hostelling International's Australia-based site.

www.yha.org.nz
Youth Hostel Association of New Zealand.

www.yha.org.uk
Youth Hostel Association of England and Wales.

Hotels

www.ase.net
www.bookeurohotels.co.uk
www.hotelmaster.co.uk
www.hotelnet.co.uk
www.usahotelguide.com

INDEPENDENT TRAVEL AND BACKPACKING

Backpacker travel sites offer helpful advice and details of hostel accommodation. They often provide facilities for on-line communities to share information.

www.backpackers.com.au
www.backpackeurope.com

www.eurotrip.com
www.nomads-backpackers.com
www.packontheback.com
www.thebackpacker.net

STUDENT TRAVEL

www.isiccard.com
www.istc.org
www.statravel.co.uk
www.usitcampus.co.uk

NATIONAL TRAVEL PORTALS
Australia

www.atn.com.au
www.australia.com
www.istc.org
www.tntmag.com.au
www.toxiccustard.com/australia
www.travelaustralia.com.au
www.travelmate.com.au

New Zealand

www.innz.co.nz
www.nztvl.com
www.purenz.com
www.tourism.net.nz
www.travelplanner.co.nz
www.travelsite.co.nz
www.webcam.co.nz
www.zedontheweb.co.nz

South Africa

www.southafrica.net
www.southafricatraveler.com
www.wildnetafrica.com

United Kingdom

www.alltraveluk.com
www.aboutbritain.com
www.britainexpress.com
www.britannia.com
www.knowhere.co.uk
www.ukguide.org
www.visitscotland.com

United States

www.travelingusa.com
www.usatourism.com
www.usatourist.com
www.welcometotheusa.net
www.worldweb.com

Other country travel sites

www.caribbean-on-line.com
Travel site for the Caribbean islands.

www.greekisland.co.uk
Digital postcards from the Greek Islands.

www.greektravel.com
Independent travel guide to Greece and the Greek Islands.

www.indo.com
Bali and Indonesia travel portal.

www.irelandseye.com
Webzine about Ireland, including travel features.

www.mexonline.com
Online Guide to Mexico.

www.polishworld.com
Directory and links for Poland.

GENERAL TRAVEL INFORMATION

www.budgettravel.com
Not the best looking site in the world, but packed with useful information and links.

www.responsibletravel.com
Interesting site promoting responsible eco-travel that benefits travellers, hosts and environments.**Ⓕ**

Other

www.mytravelguide.com
www.nationalgeographic.com
www.sitesatlas.com
www.travelfinders.com
www.travel-library.com
www.travelnotes.org
www.travigator.com
www.virtualtourist.com

TRAVEL GUIDEBOOKS

www.fodors.com
www.frommers.com
www.letsgo.com
www.lonelyplanet.com
www.roughguides.co.uk
www.timeout.com

TRAVEL RESOURCES
Currency converters

www.eurocheapo.com/currency.asp
www.oanda.com/converter/classic
www.xe.com/ucc

Embassies

www.embpage.org
Travel, trade, diplomacy and international affairs.

Maps

NATIONAL STREET AND LOCATION MAPS

Australia

www.whereis.com.au

United Kingdom

www.easymap.co.uk
When it works, it's quite good for UK street maps.

www.old-maps.co.uk
Old maps, but up-to-the-minute site providing online access to Britain's most extensive digital historical map archive, owned by the UK national mapping agency Ordnance Survey.

www.ordsvy.gov.uk
All sorts of maps of Britain from Ordnance Survey, including traditional walking and road maps, large-scale and digital maps. Plus map reading explanations and hints.**ⓕ**

www.streetmap.co.uk
Extremely useful e-mailable street maps for the UK's towns and cities.

United States

mapsonus.switchboard.com
Maps On Us provides quickly drawn maps and routes and links to Switchboard.com's 'what's nearby' facility.

nationalatlas.gov
America's natural and sociocultural landscapes as mapped by the US government.

www.mapblast.com
Interactive maps and driving instructions.

www.mapquest.com
Useful roadmaps and driving directions. Links to Mapquest sites for France, Germany and the UK.

www-nmd.usgs.gov
United States Geological Survey national mapping information.

www.topozone.com
Topographical maps for the US.

www.triscape.com
This service requires map reading software to be downloaded to your computer.

Europe

www.mappy.co.uk
Multi-language travel planner for Europe.

www.multimap.com
This is one of the most popular map sites on the Web and offers easy search street maps for European towns and cities.**ⓕ**

WORLD MAPS

www.atlapedia.com
Full colour physical and political world maps, together with statistical and historical country information.

www.lib.utexas.edu/maps
Extensive collection of online maps from the University of Texas, plus excellent links to other mapping resource sites.**ⓕ**

www.maps.com
Popular general mapping site, including trip planning facilities and a map and travel store.

Tourist information offices

www.towd.com
Searchable link site to tourism offices worldwide.

Links: Country Information

WebStuff

This section lists those sites providing information or services about topics directly relevant to the Web, including Internet and Web information, filters, WebMail, search engines and directories, domain name registration, WebCams and WebLogs.

INTERNET AND WEB NEWS AND INFORMATION

Technological developments on the Internet progress at an astounding rate. These sites will help you keep up with events.

hotwired.lycos.com
Web technology and culture.

slashdot.org
E-mail posted news for nerds.

www.dailyrotation.com
Tailorable WebLog of Internet-related technology site headlines from around the world.

www.elpub.org
Electronic Publishing research and development news and resources.

www.europemedia.net
Distilled new media information from around Europe.

www.internet.com
Internet news and information.

www.netimperative.com
UK Internet industry information provider.

www.netmag.co.uk
Online site of the respected popular UK Internet magazine.

www.nua.ie
Internet trends and statistics.

www.redherring.com
Analysis and commentary about technology.

www.wired.com
News of the digital world.

www.zdnet.com
Informative technology portal with international versions.❶

DOMAIN REGISTRATION

The domain name is the address of a Website. So it's clear who owns which name, their use is controlled and regulated. Top level domain names need to be registered with a Registry to become operational. Domain names are licensed for a renewable agreed period. There are 239 top-level country domains and most countries have a central registry to store each unique domain name. Registration is usually carried out on behalf of the user by an agent. The level of service varies, but most companies offering registration facilities also usually provide Website hosting and forwarding, e-mail forwarding, and other Internet services.

Registrars
www.afilias.info
Official registry for the new domain .info.

www.icann.org
Internet Corporation for Assigned Names and Numbers.

www.nominet.net
Registry for .uk domain names, including a long membership list of UK companies offering domain name registration services.

Registration services
Here's a small sample selection of companies offering domain registration and other Internet services. There are many others.

www.easyspace.co.uk
www.netbenefit.com
www.netnames.com
www.register.com

FILTERS, BLOCKERS AND WASHERS

There's concern that computers are being used to invade privacy by unscrupulous marketing companies, authority observers, corporations and others. Similarly, the availability of all sorts of pornographic material on the Internet is also a cause for concern. A range of software products has been designed to tackle these issues. The problem is that it's often difficult to assess the effectiveness of many of these products – do they actually work? These products play on our fears, and sales tactics often work up these fears to question the efficacy of other products on the market. If you think you need these products, buy and use them with caution.

Ad blockers

Products that keep Websites ad-free by blocking banner ads and those annoying pop-ups.

www.adfilter.co.uk
www.adsubtract.com

Internet filters and child protection

These packages purport to keep porn and other unwanted material off computers in organisations, and to protect children from the seedier side of the Net. They can usually be tailored by the user to specify subjects and levels of filtering. They build upon the protection already offered by filters integral to Internet browsers. Internet Explorer's content filter is accessed from the toolbar under Internet Options, Content. There are now many of these packages available. Here's a small selection:

www.chatdanger.com
www.cyberangels.org
www.cybersitter.com
www.netnanny.com
www.surfcontrol.com
www.webwasher.com

SEARCH ENGINES AND DIRECTORIES

This section lists a selection of general worldwide search engines and directories, rather than search facilities tailored to specific subjects such as shopping, or limited to a particular region, such as a country.

There are now hundreds of general search engines on the Net. Many offer combined directory and search facilities. The directory element subdivides information into categories, such as Art or Food and Drink, and then performs limited searches within that category. Side by side with this are often general searches that will explore the whole of the Web. If one resource doesn't deliver the desired results, then it's worth trying others, as one search engine rarely delivers the same hits as another.

about.com
directhit.com
dmoz.org
hotbot.lycos.com
www.alltheweb.com
www.altavista.com
www.askjeeves.com
www.copernic.com **❻**
www.dogpile.com
www.excite.com
www.galaxy.com
www.google.com
www.icqit.com

www.infospace.com
www.infotiger.com
www.looksmart.com
www.mamma.com
www.overture.com
www.teoma.com
www.webcrawler.com
www.webtop.com
www.zensearch.com

WEBCAMS

There's an abundance of these put to various uses throughout the Web, including JamCams which observe the traffic flow, and wildlife observation cams. The sophistication of the cameras varies. Most are static views with refreshes every minute or so, but the more exciting cams allow zoom and direction control. The following three sites provide links to a huge number of WebCams across the world.

chili.rt66.com/ozone/countries.htm❻
www.flyonthewall.tv
www.leonardsworlds.com

Links: Nature/Animal Information
Transport/United Kingdom/London
Transport/United States/Road

WEBMAIL

There are many sources from which to get free Web-based e-mail addresses. WebMail offers a convenient way of being able to pick up e-mails via computers logged onto the Net wherever you are. Here are a few of the services available.

www.another.com
www.anymail.co.za
www.emailaddresses.com

www.eudoramail.com
www.hotmail.com
www.ultimateemail.com
www.webmail.co.za

Spam

Spam is the mass of unsolicited e-mails, making all sorts of special commercial offers you don't need or want, which congests e-mail inboxes. Thankfully, many ISP and WebMail providers now manage to block much unwanted mail before it gets to the user, saving us all from drowning in a sea of spam.

www.caube.org.au
Coalition Against Unsolicited Bulk Email, Australia.

www.cauce.org
Coalition Against Unsolicited Commercial Email.

www.euro.cauce.org/en
European Coalition Against Unsolicited Commercial Email.

www.spamcon.org
Includes the Spamcon Law Center.

www.spamfree.org
Forum for Responsible and Ethical Email.

OTHER ANTI-SPAM SITES

spamcop.net
www.junkbusters.com
www.spam.abuse.net
www.spamkiller.com
www.whew.com

WEBLOGS

WebLogs are the results of personal trawlings of the Web drawn together in one central place, with links to sites plus commentary, and possibly some personal essays. They range from the enlightening to the direly self-indulgent.

portal.eatonweb.com
www.blogger.com
www.blogspot.com
www.drudgereport.com
www.obscurestore.com
www.robotwisdom.com

Women

Many of these sites are glossy emulations of women's magazines, covering the predictable topics of cosmetics, fashion, cooking, dieting, parenting, relationships, shopping and so on, with the inevitable commercial tie-ins. Other less mainstream sites tackle women's policy issues, and there are a number of friendship sites.

NEW ZEALAND

www.mwa.govt.nz
The incongruously entitled Ministry of Women's Affairs, New Zealand.

www.ncwnz.co.nz
National Council of Women – education, opinions, representation.

www.nzwomen.com
Online network for New Zealand women.

www.on-line.co.nz
New Zealand's Women's Weekly online guide.

UNITED KINGDOM

www.womens-institute.co.uk
National Federation of Women's Institutes, the UK's largest women's organisation.

www.womenwelcomewomen.org.uk
WWW on the www. Women's international friendship organisation. Members in Antarctica wanted!

Other

www.femail.co.uk
www.handbag.com
www.ivillage.co.uk

UNITED STATES

www.ivillage.com
Important portal to a large number of individual mainstream
women's sites, including *Cosmopolitan*.

www.iwpr.org
Institute for Women's Policy Research.

www.now.org
National Organization for Women.

Other

www.cybergrrl.com
www.femina.com
www.feminist.com

www.feminist.org
www.internationalwoman.net
www.marthastewart.com
www.millenniumwomen.net
www.whymenare.com
www.womensforum.com

Links: Health/Women's Health

Douglas Adams 1952–2001: An Appreciation

'You'd better be prepared for the jump into hyperspace. It's unpleasantly like being drunk.'

'What's so unpleasant about being drunk?'

'You ask a glass of water.'

from The Hitch-hiker's Guide to the Galaxy

Just over a decade ago I had the good fortune to attend a talk given by Douglas Adams during a technology conference at the Prudential Center in Boston. It was the first lecture of an early morning session on the last half-day of a demanding and stressful week-long trade show.

It is a measure of how important it was to me to hear what he had to say that I was there at all, as I had spent much of the previous evening and most of that morning demob-happy on the shores of Cape Cod, having driven down there on a whim with a few colleagues to watch the sun rise over the Atlantic. Without sleep and therefore fighting tiredness, on the cusp of 8 a.m. I had dragged myself through the shower and into crumpled smart-casuals, and made it to the Center just in time to take my seat on the third row.

Fortunately, and as anticipated, Douglas's talk was as entertaining and enlightening as his many books, radio transmissions and TV programmes. The conference was showcasing a new hypertext product from the company I was working for at the time. Douglas was the obvious choice to encourage stragglers to attend the final hurdle of the conference. His enthusiasm was infectious and his sense of humour provoked waves of appreciation through the audience. I left feeling more confident about the future of our product than perhaps, with hindsight, I should have done. As it happens, the product itself turned out to be relatively short-lived, but it signalled the emergence of the hand-held personal organisers that are ubiquitous today.

I vividly remember hearing the radio version of *The Hitch-hiker's Guide to the Galaxy* and then seeing the television version some twenty years ago. As I watched and listened again recently when the programmes were replayed by the BBC as a tribute to Douglas, *Hitch-hiker's* was confirmed as an important influence for me personally, as I suspect it was for many others. I was struck by the well documented pre-science of Douglas in creating the famous guidebook, which, of course, has clear parallels with the Net and the Web. His depiction of graphics, video and hyperlinks within a handy carry-around package which taps in to vast reservoirs of information heralds laptops, groupware, e-books and hand-held devices.

During April 2001, one of Douglas's projects, a four-part BBC Radio 4 series, *The Hitch-hiker's Guide to the Future*, situated the Internet in an everyday context, demystifying it and placing it in a developmental communications cycle. As always, his analogies and explanations opened technology up to a new audience, as he examined what advances might be made in the future, as well as humorously highlighting some of the Net's paradoxes and absurdities. It reminded me of his enlightening talk in Boston. At the time of writing, you can still catch it at the BBC Radio 4 Website shown below.

So long, Douglas. You will be sadly missed by many of us out here. Goodbye, and thanks for all the insights.

Douglas Adams's books are available via most Internet and high street bookstores. The following is a small selection of the many Websites connected with his work:

my.linkbaton.com/bibliography/adams/douglas
www.americanatheist.org/win98-99/T2/silverman.html
www.bbc.co.uk/cult/hitchhikers
www.bbc.co.uk/h2g2/guide
www.bbc.co.uk/radio4/hitchhikers

www.douglasadams.com
www.edge.org/documents/adams_index.html
www.floor42.com
www.happy-adams-day.net
www.zz9.org

APPENDICES

Shorthand

These are commonly used phrases reduced to the acronymic form.
They are designed to make messages quicker to write.

A/M	Above Mentioned
A/S/L	Age/Sex/Location
ADN	Any Day Now
AFAIK	As Far As I Know
AFK	Away From Keyboard
AKA	Also Known As
AMBW	All My Best Wishes
AOLer	A member of AOL
ASAP	As Soon As Possible
AYSOS	Are You Stupid Or Something
B4	Before
BBIAB	Be Back In A Bit
BBL	Be Back Later
BCNU	Be Seein' You
BD	Big Deal
BFD	Big F***ing Deal
BFN	Bye For Now
BIF	Basic In Fact
BITD	Back In The Day
BM	Byte Me
BRB	Be Right Back
BTSOOM	Beats The Shit Out Of Me
BTW	By The Way
CID	Consider It Done
CIO	Check It Out
Cof$	Church of Scientology

CUL8R	See You Later
CYA	See Ya
DILLIGAS	Do I Look Like I Give A Shit
DLTM	Don't Lie To Me
EML	Evil Manic Laugh
F2F	Face to Face
FUBAR	F***** Up Beyond All Recognition
FUD	(Spreading) Fear, Uncertainty, and Disinformation/Doubt
FWIW	For What It's Worth
FYA	For Your Amusement
FYI	For Your Information
GDM8	G'day mate
GG	Good Game
GL	Good Luck
GMTA	Great Minds Think Alike
GR&D	Grinning Running And Ducking
GR8	Great
GTG	Got To Go
GTGB	Got To Go, Bye
GTSY	Glad To See Ya
HAGO	Have A Good One
HTH	Hope This (or That) Helps
IAE	In Any Event
IC	In Character
IDKY	I Don't Know You
IDST	I Didn't Say That
IDTS	I Don't Think So
IFU	I F***** Up
IMHO	In My Humble Opinion
IMNSHO	In My Not So Humble Opinion
IMO	In My Opinion
IOH	I'm Outta Here
IOW	In Other Words
IRL	In Real Life
IYSS	If You Say So
IYSWIM	If You See What I Mean

KIT	Keep In Touch
L8R	Later
LMAO	Laughing My Ass Off
LOL	Laughing Out Loud -or- Lots Of Love
LTNS	Long Time No See
MHOTY	My Hat's Off To You
MorF	Male or Female
MOTD	Message Of The Day
MOTSS	Members Of The Same Sex
NBIF	No Basis In Fact
NFW	No F***ing Way
NP	No Problem
NRG	Energy
NRN	No Reply Necessary
NW	No Way
OIC	Oh, I see
OMAS	Oh My Aching Sides
OOC	Out Of Character
OOTB	Out Of The Box -or- Out Of The Blue
OTOH	On The Other Hand
PBT	Pay Back Time
PLS	Please
PMFJI	Pardon Me For Jumping In
POV	Point Of View
ROTFL	Rolling On The Floor Laughing
RSN	Real Soon Now
RTFM	Read The F***ing Manual
RTM	Read The Manual
SITD	Still In The Dark
SNAFU	Situation Normal, All F***** Up
SOL	Sooner Or Later
SorG	Straight or Gay?
SUYF	Shut Up You Fool
SWDYT	So What Do You Think

TANSTAAFL	There Ain't No Such Thing As A Free Lunch
TARFU	Things Are Really F***** Up!
TEOTWAWKI	The End Of The World As We Know It
TIA	Thanks In Advance
TIAIL	Think I Am In Love
TIC	Tongue In Cheek
TTFN	Ta Ta For Now
TTT	To The Top
TTYL	Talk To You Later
TX	Thanks
TYVM	Thank You Very Much
unPC	unPolitically Correct
WAG	Wild Ass Guess
WB	Welcome Back
WCA	Who Cares Anyway
WDYS	What Did You Say
WEG	Wicked Evil Grin
WTF	What The F***?
WTG	Way To Go!
WYRN	What's Your Real Name?
WYS	Whatever You Say
WYSIWYG	What You See Is What You Get
WYT	Whatever You Think
YA	Yet Another
YDKM	You Don't Know Me
YSYD	Yeah, Sure You Do
YTTT	You Telling The Truth?
YW	You're Welcome

Emoticons (aka Smileys)

Emoticons are a sequence of ASCII characters originally meant to represent emotion in e-mail or news (which they still do, but there are also 'emoticons' that represent things other than emotions) and usually follow after the punctuation (or in place of the punctuation) at the end of a sentence. They can be 'seen' better if the head is tilted to the left – the colon represents the eyes, the dash represents the nose and the right parenthesis represents the mouth. It should also be pointed out that they look best in the Times New Roman font.

Below is a selection of the many emoticons that have been invented. These have been split into categories depending on what they are intended to display to make them easier to view. Most are rarely used but give a strong impression of the power of the imagination and indeed the need to stay human in computing. If you are hungry for more, a search on any decent search engine should deliver the results to satiate any appetite.

States of mind

:-)	Smile
;-)	Smile with a wink
:-ll	Angry
:-(	Sad
:-))	Really happy
:-D	Big grin
:-o	Surprise/shock
$-)	Greedy
:-/	Perplexed
?:-/	Puzzlement or confusion
=:O	Frightened (hair standing on end)
=8O	Wide-eyed with fright
:-}	Embarrassed smile
;-^)	Tongue in cheek
%*@:-(	Hung over
#-)	User partied all night
<:I	Dunce

:-I	Non-committal
(-_-)	Secret smile
>:)	Perplexed look

Physical descriptions

:-)</////////>	User wearing a necktie
:-'l	User has a cold
:-~)	User has a cold
:-{}	User wearing heavy lipstick
:-)8	User is well dressed
8:-)	Glasses on forehead
{(:-)	User is wearing a toupee
(:-I	Bald person

Actions

:-*	A kiss
:-P~	A lick
X=	Fingers crossed
:-P	Sticking out a tongue
X-)	I see nothing
:-X	I'll say nothing
:-~~~	Drooling
...---...	SOS
:' -(	Crying

People/characters

(_8-(l)	Homer Simpson
Cl:-=	Charlie Chaplin
=l:-)=	Abraham Lincoln
*<:-)	Father Christmas
(:)-)	Scuba diver
*#:-)	Scotsman
0:-)	Angel
:-[	Vampire
+-:-l	Religious person
]:-)	Devil

Objects/animals

[:-I]	A robot
(:V)	A duck
3:-o	A cow
@]-'---,--	A rose
:8)	A pig
8)	A frog
>[]	A television
(::[]::)	A plaster/bandaid (can indicate help or assistance)
0>>	Ice-cream cone
<3	A heart

Assicons

These are a variation on the emoticon theme and involve a particular part of the body. Likewise, they are intended to be fun, offering a modicum of relief to those involved in the drudgery of text messaging.

(_!_)	a normal ass
(__!__)	a fat ass
(!)	a tight ass
(_._)	a flat ass
(_o^^o_)	a wise ass
(_E=mc2_)	a smart ass
(_13_)	an unlucky ass
(_$_)	money coming out of his ass
(_?_)	a dumb ass

Error Messages

When receiving any error messages, it is always worth attempting the action again one or two times. Another option is to try refreshing the page.

ERROR MESSAGE	MEANING	ACTION
400 – Bad request	Incorrect URL entered. Either the server doesn't recognise the document, the page no longer exists or access is unauthorised.	Check the entered URL for any typos. Is the address case sensitive?
401 – Unauthorised	Either the user is unauthorised or the password they entered was incorrect.	Re-enter the password.
403 – Forbidden	User is not permitted to access the document. A password may be needed.	Re-enter the password.
404 – Not found	The host server is unable to locate the file entered at the given URL. Either it has been entered incorrectly or no longer exists.	Check the entered URL for any typos. Check the site that is supposed to contain the file still exists.

550 – xxxx is not a known user	A sent e-mail wasn't recognised by the recipient mail server. Either the username part of the e-mail was incorrect or an account is no longer held with that server.	Check the e-mail's username for any typos. Is it case sensitive?
Bad file request	The form being accessed either contains an error or is not supported by the user's browser (very rare).	The user should try using a different browser.
Failed DNS lookup	The URL requested couldn't be translated into a valid Web address.	The system might've made a mistake (common) so a simple reload would correct this. Check the URL for typos.
Host unavailable	The host server may be offline or down.	Try the server again and if unsuccessful, try again later.
Unable to locate host	As above or the user has lost connection.	Re-connect if necessary and follow the instructions above.
Unable to locate server	The URL entered is either incorrect or no longer exists.	Check the URL and try again.

Host unknown	Either connection has been lost somewhere or the URL is incorrect.	Re-connect if necessary, click the Reload button or check the URL for any mistakes.
NNTP server error	An error message associated with newsgroups. Either the user's server software is not working properly or the newsgroup doesn't exist.	Check the URL and try again. If unsuccessful a number of times, the user should contact their ISP as the problem is possibly theirs.
Too many users	Some sites set a limit on the number of users allowed to access it at any given time. This is to avoid slow transfer rates.	Try again when there is less traffic.
Helper application not found	The user's browser is unable to recognise the file that it is trying to download.	The option 'save to disk' should be presented. It might be possible to open the file from the computer.
File contains no data	There are no Web pages on the requested site.	Try again later and check the URL for any errors.

Also available

The Internet from A to Z

New Edition

John Cowpertwait and Simon Flynn

Know your Dongle from your Node?
Lost your Socks or your Bozo Filter?
Frustrated with Craplets? Desperate
for a Mappucino?

The Internet from A to Z is Icon's indispensable, pocket-sized introduction and dictionary of the Net. Whether you're looking for help taking those first Internet steps, or you're already connected and would like to know more, this is the book for you.

The book is divided into two interlinked sections:

- An easy-to-understand introduction explaining the World Wide Web, e-mail, chat, newsgroups and other Net features, getting you up and running quickly.

- An easy-to-use reference guide, providing explanations of over 1,000 Internet-related terms in an A to Z format, cross-linked so you can surf from entry to entry.

ISBN 1 84046 355 4

Icon Books UK £4.99
Canada $12.99
Totem Books USA $9.95